Powerful Phrases for Effective Customer Service

Over 700 Ready-to-Use Phrases and Scripts That Really Get Results

Renée Evenson

AMACOM

New York • Atlanta • Brussels • Chicago • Mexico City • San Francisco
Shanghai • Tokyo • Toronto • Washington, D.C.

This publication is designed to provide accurate and authoritative information in regard to the subject matter covered. It is sold with the understanding that the publisher is not engaged in rendering legal, accounting, or other professional service. If legal advice or other expert assistance is required, the services of a competent professional person should be sought.

Library of Congress Cataloging-in-Publication Data

Evenson, Renee, 1951–
    Powerful phrases for effective customer service : over 700 ready-to-use
phrases and scripts that really get results / Renee Evenson.
        p.   cm.
    ISBN 978-0-8144-2032-4 — ISBN 0-8144-2032-X
    1. Customer services.   2. Customer services—Terminology.   3. Customer
relations.   4. Business communication.   I. Title.
    HF5415.5.E895   2012
    658.8′12014—dc23   2012014762

About AMA
American Management Association (www.amanet.org) is a world leader in talent development, advancing the skills of individuals to drive business success. Our mission is to support the goals of individuals and organizations through a complete range of products and services, including classroom and virtual seminars, webcasts, webinars, podcasts, conferences, corporate and government solutions, business books, and research. AMA's approach to improving performance combines experiential learning—learning through doing—with opportunities for ongoing professional growth at every step of one's career journey.

Printing number
HB 08.03.2021

CONTENTS

PART II
Powerful Phrases and Scripts
for Every Situation

5 Powerful Phrases for Challenging Employee Situations   205

6 Powerful Phrases for Social Media Interactions   281

INTRODUCTION

I've spent my entire career in customer service management and over ten years writing about how to provide exceptional customer service. One of my books, *Customer Service Training 101, 2nd edition,* offers detailed training to equip you with the necessary tools to handle your customers well. But as a customer service expert, I also understand that frontline employees have to handle many situations that are far from ideal and that can't all be covered in a training book—scenarios that leave you scrambling to know what to say and do. Let's face it: *Working in the customer service field is not easy!*

What happens when you deal with customers who are demanding, rude, angry, overly analytical, overly friendly, or even intoxicated or mentally unstable? Any of these behaviors can have you searching for the right words to say and the right actions to take. Your training often eludes you when you need it most! When you deal with customers who demand unrealistic outcomes, are combative, call you names, yell, butt in while you're helping another customer, blame you for something you didn't do, or are agitated, you're likely to stumble as you attempt to regroup, recover, and move on. As a service provider, it's your job to give great service to every one of your customers but you know it's often difficult to achieve. And, sometimes, it isn't the customer who behaves badly.

What happens when you inadvertently say or do something that causes a customer to become upset or angry? Perhaps you said something patronizing, sarcastic, tactless, or embarrassing. You realize your blunder and wish you could take back the remark, but you can't. So you don't say anything. Or you say something that makes the situation worse. And what about those situations in which you have no clue what the customer is talking about, or perhaps you were distracted and didn't listen to your customer? You wish you knew what to say to get back on track, but you don't say anything, hoping you'll figure out how to handle the interaction.

It's because of these less than ideal situations that I wrote this book. What if you developed the skills and knew the right words to say to handle any challenging behavior or situation and get the customer on your side? This would enable you to complete the interaction by finding the best solution to the situation quickly, correctly, and with a great attitude. What if you developed the skills to quickly recover when you've made a blunder with a customer? What if you knew the right words to say to diffuse any situation and maintain control of the conversation? *Powerful Phrases for Effective Customer Service* provides the necessary tools to do all that. It includes *over 700 phrases and scripts* that you'll be able to put to use in your work environment and that will give you the ability to effectively handle *30 different challenging customer behaviors and 20 challenging employee situations.*

Part I, Powerful Phrases + Actions = Successful Customer Interactions, focuses on two critical components of service: the value of using powerful phrases that communicate welcome, courtesy, rapport, enthusiasm, assurance, empathy, regret, and appreciation, and the importance of backing up your words with appropriate actions. These chapters will give you the ammunition to develop the skills and form the habit of incorporating powerful phrases and actions into your daily interactions with customers.

Part II, Powerful Phrases and Scripts for Every Situation, first focuses on the basics of typical customer interactions. You'll learn the six steps to interacting with your customers successfully. Once you learn these steps, you're ready to get to the gist of this book: learning the powerful phrases and scripts for handling challenging customer behaviors and challenging employee situations. You'll learn how to identify the behavior or situation, read a *Do This!* scenario that reinforces the correct method for dealing with it, and get an explanation of *Why This Works.* You'll learn how to apply the approach to your particular work environment and your customers. You'll even learn how to effectively interact with customers who post comments, complaints, or compliments on social media sites.

This is the book you'll keep handy. It's the book you'll turn to when you need to know how to work with a challenging customer. It's the book you'll use when you realize you've said or done something wrong and need to know how to conduct yourself differently in the future. It's the book that will give you the confidence to handle any type of customer behavior and any situation that may have previously caused you to stumble. It's the book that will help you deal not only with customers, but also with vendors, suppliers, potential customers, coworkers, upper management, and your competition. Any time you enter into a give and take interaction, the person you're speaking to can be considered your customer, even if that person is a family member or a friend. *Powerful Phrases for Effective Customer Service* is the book that will give you the tools you need to conduct yourself well in any interaction.

ACKNOWLEDGMENTS

My sincere and heartfelt thank you to each of you for helping me as I wrote this book:

My editor, Bob Nirkind, for suggesting I write this book. Thanks also for your involvement, input, and interest as we worked through the process. I can't tell you how much fun I've had working on this project.

My agent, Michael Snell, for being my voice and keeping my best interests at heart.

My production editor, Barbara Chernow and her associates, for always teaching me something new and reteaching the old that I continue to forget.

My husband and proofreader, Joe Balka, who gave me honest feedback and helpful advice when reading this manuscript.

My clients, friends, and family who gave me input for the behaviors and scenarios in this book. Thanks for all your help.

My deepest appreciation goes to each of you reading this book.

PART I

Powerful Phrases + Actions = Successful Customer Interactions

1

Communicating Powerful Phrases

***Customer Service means finding the best
solution for each customer, quickly,
correctly, and with a helpful attitude.***

The above goal might be easy to accomplish when you're handling those easy-to-satisfy, pleasant customers, but let's face it: Many customers are not easily satisfied. And they're not always pleasant. In fact, they're often hurried, stressed out, impatient, demanding, or downright rude; no one, it seems, has the time for all the niceties of interpersonal interaction anymore. We live in a society where instant gratification is the norm. Customers want service and they want it now. Not later, not when it's convenient for you. NOW!

As a service provider, it's your job to give your customers great service, but you know that it's often difficult to do. Dealing with customers can be challenging. They may leave you feeling frustrated, stressed out, angry, or visibly upset. They can sometimes leave you scrambling for the right words to say. They will occasionally flabbergast you to the point where you go blank and can't think of an appropriate response. And there are times when you completely regret the words that have flown out of your mouth. Knowing what to say when handling different types of customer behaviors is anything but easy.

The truth is, the customer is *not* always right. But . . . when you work in the service field, it's your job to be courteous, respectful, and helpful, even when those behaviors aren't exhibited by your customers. And, although customers may not always be right, it's their perceptions of good service that matters and it's how they're being treated that's important to them. You only succeed at providing exceptional service when your customers believe they've received exceptional service.

What if you possessed the skills to handle the less than ideal behaviors that some customers, and, at times, even you may display? What if you knew how to quickly identify bad behavior and maintain control of the conversation? What if you knew the right words to say to diffuse any situation and professionally handle every customer to his or her satisfaction?

Using powerful phrases—the right words—when you communicate gives you the confidence that you're communicating your best. As a result, your customers' perceptions of service will be positive. It's all about the words you choose. What you say can make all the difference in how your customers view you and your company.

Starting every customer interaction with a welcoming phrase helps put your best foot forward. By speaking courteously, respectfully, and enthusiastically, you foster an open dialogue with your customers. Building a rapport and showing that you're interested helps to make every interaction go smoothly. When appropriate, adding powerful phrases that convey empathy or regret indicate that you are genuinely concerned and truly understand the other person's point of view. Ending every customer contact with powerful phrases of appreciation leaves a positive impression in any customer's mind.

As you read this chapter, you're going to learn helpful powerful phrases that will make every customer interaction end successfully, especially those that didn't start that way, whether it was you or your customer who behaved badly. Make the use of powerful phrases a habit, a part of your everyday vocabulary, and you'll successfully handle every customer confidently and maintain control of any situation.

Don't Do This!

Linda is a receptionist in a physician's office. Her responsibilities include greeting and checking in patients, answering the phone, and scheduling appointments. The morning had been unusually stressful for her. Earlier, the doctor was called to the hospital to perform emergency surgery and is now running approximately an hour behind in seeing office patients.

While Linda was busy phoning patients to reschedule appointments affected by the delay, she was also dealing with patients in the waiting room, many of whom were becoming impatient. She was on a telephone call when she noticed that one of the patients who had been waiting almost an hour was standing at the window to the reception area. Linda did not make eye contact, but rather stared at her computer screen until she finished her phone call.

She slid the window open. "Yeah?" she asked, with no emotion showing on her face.

"I've been waiting almost an hour now," the patient responded. "Do you have any idea how long it's going to be?"

"I told you when you checked in that the doctor's running behind," Linda answered in an annoyed tone. "I have no idea how long it'll be. Do you want to wait or reschedule?"

"Well, I'm here. The same thing could happen next time. I have no choice but to wait," the patient replied, mocking Linda's annoyed tone. Linda slid the window closed and picked up the phone to call the next patient on her list.

Why This Doesn't Work

Linda's interaction with the patient didn't work because she didn't choose the correct words. Powerful phrases could have made all the difference! When she slid the window open, she said one word, Yeah?, in a tone that signaled she felt bothered. Linda could have used a powerful phrase that was welcoming, such as asking in an interested tone, *How may I help you?* which would have gotten the conversation off on a more positive note. When she failed to empathize with the patient about the lengthy wait and then spoke in a chastising manner, the patient became annoyed. Choosing powerful phrases that show regret and compassion, such as, *I'm sorry that you've been waiting so long. I understand that you've probably got other things to do today,* and then following up with a statement of appreciation, such as *I appreciate your patience,* would have shown the patient that she cared.

Had Linda incorporated powerful phrases into the dialogue, she would have paved the way to a successful interaction. Linda's choice of words left the patient less than pleased, and she likely didn't feel very positive about their conversation either.

Phrases of Welcome

The first words you say to customers can welcome them into your business, giving them a sense of warmth and friendliness, or they can make your customers feel so uncomfortable that they want to leave. The temperature of your words can either be warm and inviting or cold and unwelcoming. It's your choice. When you choose phrases of welcome, you open the door wide and increase your chances of successful customer interactions.

Sample Phrases of Welcome

Offering a warm welcome to your customers helps break the ice, helps your customer begin forming a positive impression of you, and helps to create an atmosphere of comfort.

- *"Hello/Hi!"*
- *"Good morning/afternoon/evening!"*
- *"Welcome to _____!"*
- *"Thank you for calling _____. My name is___."*
- *"Hi, Mr./Ms. _____. It's great to see you again."*
- *"I'm pleased to meet you."* (When introduced to a customer)
- *"My name is _____."* (Offer when appropriate)
- *"How may I help you?"*
- *"What can I help you with today?"*
- *"Can I help you find something?"*
- *"May I help you with that?"*

Incorporating Phrases of Welcome

Always be the first to greet your customers; they should never have to greet you first or ask for help. Offer a warm welcome to show your customers you're happy they chose your business. Include in your welcoming phrase an offer to help. For example: *"Hi. Welcome to Pete's Patio Shop! How can I help you today?"* If your company has a standard greeting, add a phrase of welcome to personalize the greeting. When you use these phrases and speak enthusiastically, it indicates your eagerness to help. Sound like you truly are interested in being of assistance. Show that you're pleased the customer chose your business. Even when their demeanor or facial expression is less than congenial, it's your job to welcome them into your business and make them feel comfortable. Using phrases of welcome can improve even a negative person's attitude.

Powerful Phrases Make the Difference

Phrase: You walk into a store and spot a clerk behind the counter. She looks at you and asks in a bored tone, "Do you need anything?" You can't help but wonder why she bothered asking.

Powerful Phrase of Welcome: You walk into a store and spot a clerk behind the counter. She looks at you, smiles, and enthusiastically says, "*Hi! How are you?*"

You reply, "I'm doing great, thanks."

She smiles, nods, and asks, "*How may I help you today?*" You return the smile, feeling comfortable that you came into this store.

Phrases of Courtesy

After welcoming customers into your place of business, how you handle the remainder of your interaction indicates how you view your customers, as well as how you view yourself. Customers appreciate being treated courteously, so when you interject words and phrases of courtesy appropriately throughout your conversations, you show your customers that you respect them. Using phrases of courtesy can also help you promote a positive first impression and keep you on track to build a rapport with your customers. When you form the habit of using these phrases, they'll become a natural part of the vocabulary you consistently use.

Sample Phrases of Courtesy

Below are some examples of common courtesies that should be a part of your normal vocabulary with customers as well as with all others.

- *"Please."*
- *"Thank you."*
- *"You're welcome."*
- *"Excuse me/Pardon me"* (When you didn't hear or when you need to ask the person to move.)
- *"I apologize. I didn't hear/understand what you said."*, or *"I'm sorry, I need to pass by."*
- *"Will you?"* rather than *"You will."*
- *"Yes,"* rather than *"Yeah."*
- *"Sir."*
- *"Ma'am."*
- *"I'll check and be right back."*
- *"Will you hold for a moment while I check on that?"*
- *"Thanks for waiting."*
- *"Mr./Mrs./Ms. _____."*) Address by first name only if you know that's appropriate)

Incorporating Phrases of Courtesy

Using *please*, *thank you*, and *you're welcome* shouldn't need any explanation, yet it seems these words, especially *thank you*, are seldom used anymore. Your customers will appreciate hearing these courtesies and a heartfelt *thank you* will go a long way. When you don't understand someone, Huh? will make your point, but saying *Pardon me, Excuse me,* or *I'm sorry, I didn't hear what you said,* comes across more professionally. Likewise, if you need to move by someone, prefacing your request with *Pardon me* or *Excuse me* indicates courtesy. Choose *yes* rather than *yeah* because it sounds better. *Sir* and *Ma'am* are signs of respect, but make sure to say them in a respectful rather than a condescending tone. When you need to leave the customer to check something or place the customer on hold, explain what you're doing. When you return, thank the customer for waiting. Lastly, people enjoy hearing their names, so if you know your customer's name, interject it into your conversation.

Powerful Phrases Make the Difference

Phrase: You're in a home improvement store and can't find what you're looking for. You ask an employee, "Do you carry electrical boxes?" The employee looks up and says, "Huh?" You repeat the question. He replies, "Yeah, they're in Aisle 2," then turns and walks away. You walk to Aisle 2 and, still having a problem locating what you need, wish the employee had shown you where to find them.

Powerful Phrase of Courtesy: You ask an employee, "Do you carry electrical boxes?" The employee looks up, smiles, and says apologetically, *"I'm sorry, I didn't hear what you asked."* You repeat the question, to which he replies, *"Yes,* we do carry them. You'll find them in Aisle 2 next to the wiring supplies. In fact, I'm going that way. Why don't I show you where to find them?"

Phrases of Rapport

When you welcome customers into your business and show respect by using phrases of courtesy, you set the stage to establish a rapport.

This means finding common ground, or a starting point, for a conversation about something you and another person can relate to. Show your customers from the start of your conversation that you're friendly and interested in them. They'll see that you're approachable and that you want to help. They'll likely respond in a positive manner. Pick up on the clues you receive from your customers, and you'll find ways to begin building a rapport with them.

Sample Topics and Phrases of Rapport

You can begin establishing a rapport in many ways. Below are some sample subjects that can be used to find common ground with others.

- Current events—subjects other than politics and religion.
- Weather—*"How do you like this heat/cold/snow/rain?"*
- Sports—your customer is wearing a team logo—*"Great game last night, wasn't it?"*
- Entertainment—if you can think of something relevant either to customers or your interactions with them.
- Compliment—if you like something about your customer's appearance, offer a sincere comment—*"I like your jacket."*
- Nonverbal cues—flustered mom with crying toddler—*"I'm a mom and have been there. I'm going to take care of this as quickly as I can for you."* (This also includes a powerful phrase of empathy, and displaying empathy is a great way to build rapport).
- General—if you can't think of anything to say or can't find common ground, smile warmly and ask—*"How are you doing today?"*

Incorporating Phrases of Rapport

When you welcome your customers, listen to their opening statements, pay attention to nonverbal cues, try to pick up a clue or two to begin building a rapport. Stick to safe subjects, such as the examples above. If your customer doesn't appear to be friendly or receptive, avoid launching into what may be an unwelcome conversation. Subjects that are always and absolutely taboo are politics, religion, and giving or asking overly personal information. Keep in mind that the purpose of establishing a rapport is to help your customer see you as a warm, empathetic person. When you can't find common ground, it's always a safe bet to offer a warm smile and ask, "*How are you doing today?*"

Powerful Phrases Make the Difference

Phrase: You walk into a trendy clothing store and feel slightly ill at ease because you've heard the merchandise can be pricey. The salesperson standing behind the counter looks quite snobby. She says, "Good Morning. Let me know if I can help in any way," in an icy tone. You look around for a very short time and, feeling uncomfortable, make a quick exit.

Powerful Phrase of Rapport: Feeling slightly ill at ease, you walk into this store. The salesperson walks toward you, smiles and says, "Good Morning. Welcome to Joseph's Boutique." Then she says, "*I love your pink top. That's a great color on you.*" Her smile and compliment put you at ease. After thanking her and mentioning pink is your favorite color, she asks, "We have some great tops in pink. What can I help you find today?" You reply that you're going to look around and the employee makes casual conversation as you leisurely browse.

Phrases of Enthusiasm

Welcoming your customers, using phrases of courtesy, and establishing a rapport are important components in any interaction because they serve a critical purpose: making your customers feel comfortable and at ease in your place of business, whether they are standing in front of you, holding a telephone to their ear, or communicating with you online. But let's be honest: your customers don't come to you for the purpose of feeling comfortable and making small talk. They visit, call, or email you for a reason. They may want to make a purchase, have a question that needs to be answered, have a problem that needs to be resolved, or merely visit your business to browse. Responding to their needs enthusiastically will further their feelings of comfort when interacting with you.

Sample Phrases of Enthusiasm

These are some examples of ways in which you can show your enthusiasm when responding to your customers. How many more can you think of?

- *"I'll be happy to help!"*
- *"Yes!"*
- *"Sure!"*
- *"I can!"*
- *"Definitely!"*
- *"Absolutely!"*
- *"Let's try it!"*
- *"I like that."*
- *"That sounds great."*

Incorporating Phrases of Enthusiasm

Words and phrases of enthusiasm are meant to show your eagerness to help. There's something powerful about sending an enthusiastic, positive message: they make the recipient feel good. It's difficult saying words like *definitely* or *absolutely* in a bored or monotone voice. These and other enthusiasm words lend themselves to voicing a confident, self-assured manner. When your customers state their needs, whether it's to solve a problem or to get help finding a product, always respond with a phrase of enthusiasm to convey that you want to provide the best customer service possible. Continue use phrases of enthusiasm throughout your interactions, as appropriate.

Powerful Phrases Make the Difference

Phrase: You were recently in the hospital for minor surgery. This morning you opened your bill and can't make sense of the ten pages of charges. You call the hospital's billing department to ask for an explanation. The employee responds, "What's your account number?" You can't help but wonder how well you're going to understand the bill after speaking with this employee.

Powerful Phrase of Enthusiasm: You ask for help understanding the charges, and the employee answers, "*I'll be happy to explain the bill to you!* May I have your account number please?"

Phrases of Assurance

Many of your interactions with customers will be typical. That is, they need a product or service, and you provide what they want in the time frame and manner that suits them. Your customers then leave your place of business satisfied with their experiences. But what happens when you handle customer complaints or problems—any situation in which customers feel they have been mishandled or mistreated, experienced a miscommunication, or are just confused? In these types of situations, you want to convey something more than an enthusiastic offer to help. You want to communicate a sense of urgency and let the customer know that the buck stops with you—that you're going to take care of the problem. Offering a statement of assurance keeps you confident and in control of the conversation.

Sample Phrases of Assurance

In those instances where you want to respond in a way that shows you paid attention to your customer and conveys your understanding of the problem, use one of the following phrases.

- *"I'm going to take care of this right now."*
- *"I'm going to correct this for you immediately."*
- *"Let me check on that right now."*
- *"Let me see what happened so that I can correct it for you."*
- *"I'll check with my supervisor."*
- *"I'll get my supervisor for you."*
- *"I'm going to get you to the department that can help, and I'll stay on the line until they answer."*
- *"I'll make sure that doesn't happen again."*
- *"I'm going to refer this to my supervisor to make sure it doesn't happen in the future."*

Incorporating Phrases of Assurance

Whenever a customer comes to you with a problem that needs to be resolved, the first words out of your mouth should always include a phrase of regret, along with a phrase of assurance. You want to say something like *"I'm sorry that happened"* and follow it immediately with an assurance that you're going to help. Speaking in the affirmative, "*I'm going to take care of this right now,*" will diffuse an upset or angry customer. When you don't know what to do or if the customer adamantly refuses your help, you have no choice but to get your supervisor involved. You may either ask your supervisor to make a determination or have the supervisor speak to the customer, whichever action is appropriate. At times, you'll need to refer a customer to another employee or department. If doing so by phone, always stay on the line, introduce the customer, and explain the customer's request to the other employee before you hang up. After handling any problem situation, closing with a statement such as "*I'll make sure that doesn't happen again*" tells the customer that you care enough to take measures so this type of problem does not recur.

Powerful Phrases Make the Difference

Phrase: You call a company after finding a discrepancy on your invoice. The employee answers, "ABC Plumbing." You respond, "I just received an invoice, and it's not the same amount the man quoted when he was out to fix the problem. Can you check it for me?" "What's your account number?" You give your account number, not feeling very confident that this employee is interested in helping you.

Powerful Phrase of Assurance: The employee answers, "Thanks for calling ABC Plumbing. My name is Bob. What can I do for you today?" After asking the employee to check the invoice, he speaks in an enthusiastic manner. "Yes, Ma'am. *Let me see what happened so I can take care of this for you.* May I please have your account number?" "It's 48332." "*Thank you.* I'm pulling it up on my screen now. Other than opening this invoice and finding a discrepancy, how are you doing today?"

Phrases of Empathy

Empathy means to identify with another's feelings by relating to what they're going through. Metaphorically, it means putting on someone else's shoes and seeing a particular situation from his or her perspective. Phrases of empathy are used to show your customers that you understand what they're experiencing. Incorporating these phrases can enhance the rapport you're building with customers. They won't be appropriate in every contact, but you'll use them when you want your customers to understand that you know what they're feeling or experiencing.

Sample Phrases of Empathy Phrases

Most likely, you already use many of the following statements when speaking with family members and friends to show your understanding of a situation or an emotion. Conveying empathy with customers sends a positive message that demonstrates you're listening to them and relating to what they're telling you.

- *"I understand"* (followed by an appropriate response).
- *"I understand. I've had the same thing happen."*
- *"I'd feel the same way if that happened to me."*
- *"I can see how you feel."*
- *"I can relate . . ."*
- *"That's tough, I feel for you."*
- *"That's too bad."*
- *"I feel bad for you."*
- *"I agree completely."*

Incorporating Phrases of Empathy

Often, just letting your customers know that you understand what they're going through is the best way to show empathy. Sometimes customers will say something, looking for a response. Responding with a phrase of empathy shows them that you were paying attention. And if you don't agree with what someone says, that's fine; it's still perfectly okay to show empathy. Just letting the person know you understand his or her feelings is an important step in building rapport and strengthening relationships.

Powerful Phrases Make the Difference

Phrase: You are having an awful day. Nothing is going right. Then, when you were late picking up your son from school, you got a ticket for running a stop sign. You make a quick stop at a convenience store to buy a gallon of milk. The clerk asks how you are. You smile wearily and respond with, "I'm having a terrible day. Nothing is going right! To top it off, I got a ticket. I can't wait to just get home and take my shoes off." The clerk replies, "That'll be $5.09, please." You wonder why she bothered asking.

Powerful Phrase of Empathy: You respond to the clerk's greeting with, "I'm having a terrible day. Nothing is going right! To top it off, I got a ticket. I can't wait to just get home and take my shoes off." The clerk replies, "*I can relate! Other than getting a ticket, I had one of those days just yesterday.*"

Phrases of Regret

Phrases of regret, like phrases of empathy, show your customers that you understand what they're experiencing. They go a step beyond empathy, though, because in addition to conveying understanding, they also express sympathy or sorrow. When you've made a mistake, offer a phrase of regret. When someone else in your company made a mistake, offer a phrase of regret. Whenever a customer has a problem involving your company, offer a phrase of regret. And certainly, if the customer tells you about a personal problem, offer a phrase of regret.

Sample Phrases of Regret Phrases

Expressing regret does not come easily for many of us. Saying those two words—I'm sorry—is tough, particularly when you don't feel you need to apologize for something you didn't do. But these two words, and other phrases of regret, mean a lot to the recipient.

- *"I apologize."*
- *"I'm sorry."*
- *"I'm sorry that happened."*
- *"I made a mistake."*
- *"Please forgive me. "*
- *"I feel terrible . . ."*
- *"You'll have to excuse me . . ."*

Incorporating Phrases of Regret

Offering a sincere regret whether or not you caused the customer to become upset is always the right thing to do. Even when you don't feel that you should apologize, doing so will make your customer feel better. Just be careful to use these phrases in a sincere manner. Otherwise, you run the risk of sounding phony or sarcastic. Also, be careful not to overuse phrases of regret to avoid sounding guilty. When you don't know what to say, just saying *I'm sorry* or *I apologize* is always a good choice. Phrases of regret are often used in conjunction with phrases of assurance and empathy, as you'll see in the example below.

Powerful Phrases Make the Difference

Phrase: This is your second time calling a company about a problem on your bill. A charge was supposed to be credited this billing cycle, but when you opened your bill today you saw that it hadn't been done. You explain the situation to the employee in a frustrated manner, stressing this is the second time you're calling. The employee answers, "What's your phone number?" You wonder if the employee will really take care of the problem.

Powerful Phrase of Regret: You explain the situation to the employee in a frustrated manner, stressing this is the second time you're calling. The employee answers, "*I'm sorry about that.* I can certainly understand your frustration. Let me check on that right now and I'll make sure it's been taken care of. May I have your phone number please?"

Phrases of Appreciation

Showing customers that you appreciate them is smart business. Showing appreciation to others begins by appreciating yourself. Appreciation means to be thankful and grateful. When you feel this way, you send out positive energy to others. Incorporating phrases of appreciation into every customer contact gives your customers a sense of significance and demonstrates that they matter to you. It's human nature to want to feel valued. When you show appreciation to every customer, whether or not they actually do business with you, it will instill positive feelings in them.

Sample Phrases of Appreciation Phrases

Think about how good you feel when someone tells you they appreciate you. Think how good you feel when someone says thank you to you. Now think how good your customers are going to feel when you express your appreciation to them.

- *"I/We appreciate you."*
- *"I/We appreciate your business."*
- *"That's a great suggestion, thanks!"*
- *"I'm glad I was able to help you."*
- *"What else can I help you with?"*
- *"Was everything all right?"*
- *"Thank you for your business."*
- *"Thank you so much for calling."*
- *"Thanks for coming in."*
- *"Please stop by again."*
- *"We hope to see you soon."*
- *"Thank you."*

Incorporating Phrases of Appreciation

As you can see by these examples, there are many ways in which to express your appreciation to customers. Telling your customers that you appreciate them in a sincere manner communicates a powerful, positive message. After completing a sale, a phrase of appreciation shows that you value their business. After handling a problem, expressing your gratitude that you were able to find a workable solution conveys your appreciation for the customer's patience and understanding. And when you can't think of anything personal or unique to say, two simple words, *Thank You,* say it all.

Powerful Phrases Make the Difference

Phrase: After you finish placing a catalog order over the telephone, the employee says, "I've placed your order. The order number is 58722134. Everything is in stock and the order should go out by tomorrow." You reply, "Thank you," to which the employee says, "No problem." You hang up feeling blasé about the person you spoke to.

Powerful Phrase of Appreciation: After you finish placing a catalog order over the telephone, the employee says, "I've placed your order. The order number is 58722134. Everything is in stock and the order should go by tomorrow. *What else can I help you with today?*" You respond, "Nothing, thanks." The employee ends your conversation with, *"Thanks so much for calling. We really appreciate your business."*

Do This!

Linda was on a telephone call when she noticed that one of the patients who had been waiting almost an hour was standing at the window to the reception area. She made eye contact, slid the window open, and signaled she would be off the phone in a moment. She noticed the patient appeared angry.

She quickly ended the call, and said, *"I'm sorry, Mr. Logan, I know you've been waiting a long time. How can I help you?"* (**regret, courtesy, empathy, welcome**)

His look of anger softened into one of resignation. "It's been almost an hour now. Do you have any idea how much longer it'll be?"

"Let me check right now. . . . We have one patient in the exam room waiting to see the doctor and then you're next. I'd estimate it's going to be another fifteen minutes, though, before we can get you in." Linda looked at him sympathetically. *"I can imagine this has*

been frustrating for you and not at all how you planned your day to go." **(assurance, empathy, rapport)**

"No, it isn't," he replied, looking surprised that she seemed to know exactly how he was feeling.

"*The doctor is doing her best to see everyone today and she, too, understands this must be frustrating for all of you. If you can't wait any longer, I can reschedule you.*" **(empathy, assurance)**

"I know she's doing her best. I'll wait," Mr. Logan said and then smiled at Linda.

"*I appreciate your patience. Thank you.*" **(appreciation, courtesy)**

"No problem. Thanks for your help," Mr. Logan replied.

Why This Works

Linda understood that the delay in seeing patients could cause some of those waiting to become upset, frustrated, or even angry, and when Mr. Logan waited to see her, she identified his behavior as anger. She knew that the words she chose could either further anger him or calm him down. By choosing powerful phrases that conveyed courtesy, rapport, assurance, empathy, regret, and appreciation throughout her conversation, she was able to diffuse the patient's anger. When Linda said she understood how frustrating the situation must be for him, she showed that she truly cared and was looking at the situation from his viewpoint. Choosing powerful phrases not calmed the patient down, so that he thanked Linda for her help. They both felt good about the interaction.

2

Actions That Enhance Powerful Phrases

*Customer Service means finding the best
solution for each customer, quickly,
correctly, and with a helpful attitude.*

Why include a chapter on actions in a book about phrases? The answer is simple: Actions always speak louder than words. You can say a powerful phrase of welcome, but look disgruntled and the customer isn't going to feel welcome. You can say a powerful phrase of assurance, but say it in a tone of voice that conveys a lack of interest and the customer isn't going to have much confidence in your desire to help. And you can say a phrase of courtesy, such as "*Yes, Ma'am,*" and sound condescending. So . . . even though this book focuses on the words you say, your actions need to match what comes out of your mouth if you want to meet the goal of providing exceptional customer service.

As mentioned in Chapter 1, you only provide great service when your customers perceive they've received great service. Choosing the right words to say will achieve this goal, but act inappropriately and you'll communicate an entirely different message. This chapter focuses on showing you how to complement your words with the right actions to ensure that your customers' perceptions are positive.

You know how tough it is to give your best when your powerful phrases and actions aren't appreciated or when customers treat you badly. When you become frustrated, stressed, angry, or upset by the way you're treated, it's not only tough to think of the right phrases to say, it's even tougher to have your actions match your words. Most of us wear our feelings on our faces, our sleeves, or somewhere it's going to show! So how do you manage to say the right words and act in a manner that translates positively to customers? By remembering that it's your job to treat each customer to your best ability no matter how you're treated. So the best advice is: Don't take it personally!

Never allow other people to dump their bad behavior on you. Keep in mind that when someone treats you badly, that person may very well treat everyone that way, or perhaps the person is having a bad day and not able to control his or her emotions. This does not excuse anyone's bad behavior, but remember that bad behavior comes from what's inside that person.

To make it right, take the high road. While this can to be tough to manage in the worst of circumstances, it's your J-O-B. Think about it this way: taking the high road keeps you in control of the conversation. Taking the high road increases your confidence. Taking the high road keeps you calm. So the next time someone treats you badly, repeat to yourself: "I'm not taking it personally . . ." or "This isn't about me . . ." or "I feel sorry for this person . . ." or something that can't be written here. You get the idea. Reassuring yourself that the way someone is speaking to you isn't about you will help you stay calm.

You also know it's not always customers who treat frontline employees poorly. Sometimes it's the employee who needs an attitude adjustment. Do you know what upsets customers most when it comes to their perceptions of service? According to customers, the top reasons for poor service are employees who ignore them; don't listen to them; don't do what they say they will when they say they will; don't follow up or follow through; or aren't knowledgeable about their company's products, services, or policies.

The last reason should be easy to address. All employees should be knowledgeable when it comes to providing customer service. Unless you're knowledgeable about your products, services, and policies, you'll never achieve the goal of giving great service. You'll never be able to find the best solution for your customers unless you know what the best solution is. If you know that you need to learn more, decide what training would be most beneficial for you and ask your boss for help. Keep in mind, though, that no matter how well you're trained, situations will occur in which you won't know what to do. It may be an off-the-wall request or a situation that hasn't occurred before. If you're unsure how to handle an interaction, you can always ask for your supervisor's help.

The other reasons cited by customers for poor service can be remedied by choosing powerful phrases enhanced by powerful actions. Giving each customer your full attention, projecting a great attitude, making sure your tone and body language match your message, and acting in an ethical manner will enable you to successfully interact with every customer. Maintaining a high-energy level and using calming techniques will then help you seal the deal.

Don't Do This!

Jessica works in the women's department of a large clothing chain. It had been a slow morning, so she decided to call her best friend to chat. She was deep into her conversation and, just as she said, "I can't believe that she's still dating that jerk," she turned around to find a customer glaring at her. Looking shocked to see the woman standing there, she turned her back to the customer and whispered loudly, "I gotta go. I've got a customer waiting. I agree totally. I can't believe it either. We should probably say something to her. Look, I'll call you right back, and we can talk about what to do." Jessica turned back to the woman who was holding up a dress and said hurriedly, "I'm sorry about that. I'll ring that right up for you."

"I'm not ready to check out," the customer said in a peeved tone. "I can't find my size. Can you check to see if you have this in a size eight?"

Annoyed at the way the customer spoke to her, Jessica replied, unsmiling, "All our stock is out, Ma'am." Her tone, when saying Ma'am, sounded sarcastic, as though she was upset with the customer for being peeved. "I'll be happy to look around to see if your size is on another rack. What size did you need?" She stifled a yawn, took the dress from the customer, and walked away.

When Jessica returned, still unsmiling, she said, "I'm sorry, I looked all over but couldn't find it in an eight." She fidgeted with the cell phone in her pocket.

The customer replied, "Well, okay."

As an afterthought, Jessica asked, "Is there anything else I can help you find?"

"No thanks," the customer replied.

Jessica called her friend as the customer walked away.

Why This Doesn't Work

Although Jessica used powerful phrases of courtesy, assurance, regret, and appreciation, her actions throughout the exchange did not match her words. Her first mistake was that she was not paying attention, reasoning that since business was slow it would be all right to make a personal call. Her second mistake was not ending the call immediately when she turned around to see the customer. Instead, she showed more courtesy to her friend than to her customer. While Jessica said the right words, *I'm sorry,* and offered to ring up the customer's order right away, Jessica's attitude changed when the customer spoke in a peeved manner. She didn't smile and, although she did offer to look for the dress, her attitude reflected her annoyance and her tone in saying *Ma'am* showed sarcasm. Further, because she hadn't listened carefully, she had to ask for the correct size. When she stifled a yawn suggesting tiredness and exhibited a lack of energy, it didn't reflect well with the customer. And, though she ended the interaction with the right words, asking the customer if she could help with anything else, Jessica's actions spoke volumes as she fidgeted with her cell phone, indicating that she wanted to be done with the customer in order to get back to her personal call.

Attentiveness Is Job Number 1

The only way to deliver customer service is to pay attention to your customers. In fact, paying attention is the most important action you can take. If you aren't paying attention, you may not notice when a customer comes into your business, as in the example above. You're also not going to fully listen. And when you don't listen, you don't know how to respond appropriately or say the correct powerful phrases. When that happens, you aren't going to intuit the best solution. When you handle customers, your number one job is to pay attention to them. When you pay attention, your customers know they matter to you. When you pay attention, you're on your way to delivering great customer service. And when you pay attention, your customers will begin forming a positive impression of you.

Sample Attentiveness Actions

Your number one job is to help customers. No matter what other task you're involved with, when a customer comes in, calls, or emails you, you need to pay attention and take care of the request immediately.

- Stop whatever you are doing when a customer comes in or calls.
- Make eye contact.
- Stay fully present.
- Tune in to your customer, and tune out distractions.
- Focus entirely on the customer you're helping.
- Listen actively.
- Listen without interrupting.
- Listen for what isn't said.

Incorporating Attentiveness Actions

Your customers are the reason you have your job, which is why you should give them your complete attention. No matter what task you're involved in, when a customer comes into your business, stop, look, and listen. Stop what you're doing; tune out distractions, and focus entirely on the customer. Look at the customer, make eye contact, and smile. Listen completely so that you'll know the right powerful phrases to respond with and, most importantly, you'll know how to find the best approach for helping each customer. When you give your customers your full attention and listen completely, you demonstrate that you're interested in them and in taking care of their needs.

Powerful Actions Make the Difference

Action: You're seated at the desk of the bank employee who's answering your questions about CD rates and other interest bearing accounts. Every time the door opens, she looks to see who's coming in, and you're becoming frustrated because this throws her off track and forces her to look at her computer screen again before picking up where she left off in your conversation.

Attentiveness Action: The bank employee is doing a good job explaining the different types of accounts. Even though it's a busy morning and customers are coming and going, she looks directly at you and you only, paying attention to your conversation and making it clear that you are her priority.

A Positive Attitude Is Everything

If attentiveness is job number one, projecting a positive attitude follows closely behind. Your attitude, whether good or bad, is what customers are going to remember about their interaction with you. Think about it this way: you're the only person in charge of you. You make the decisions for and about yourself. The best decision you can make every day for yourself, as well as for others, is to present a positive face to the world. When you make the decision to maintain a positive attitude, you'll project this attitude outward and, as a result, you'll feel more positive.

Sample Attitude Actions

Attitudes rub off. When people project a negative attitude, they drag others down. Likewise, when people project a positive attitude, they lift others' spirits. People gravitate to those who appear happy, display enthusiasm, and present an upbeat attitude. No matter how you feel, presenting a positive attitude at work will help others reciprocate with a positive attitude toward you.

- Smile.
- Appreciate the good in yourself.
- Appreciate the good in others.
- Believe in yourself.
- Believe you can make a difference.

- Don't take yourself too seriously.
- Learn to laugh at yourself.
- Take the high road.
- Be interested in others.
- Do something for someone else.
- Help someone.
- Show enthusiasm.
- Choose positive words.
- If you can't say something nice . . . don't say anything!
- Keep an open mind.
- Don't stereotype.
- Stay accountable for your actions.

Incorporating Attitude Actions

No matter how you feel inside, you can project a positive face outward. Every morning use positive self-talk to create in your mind a vision of presenting a positive attitude throughout the day. When you learn to believe in yourself, that you can make a difference, you create a powerful attitude booster. When you learn not to take yourself too seriously, you can relax and enjoy the person you are. A good way to project a positive attitude is to offer to help someone, even if it's something as simple as holding a door for a stranger. When at your job, stay enthusiastic and energetic, interested in your customers and your work. Always give your best to each customer. Avoid the temptation to judge others or form stereotypes; these are attitude zappers. Remember that everyone has a bad day from time to time, so if you aren't feeling so positive today that's okay. Just make sure you keep that feeling inside. Besides, as stated above, when you project a positive attitude you start feeling more positive.

Powerful Actions Make the Difference

Action: You're interested in buying a new computer and head over to the local office supply store. You walk to the area where the computers are displayed and notice two salespeople arranging software on a shelf. They're having a good time laughing and joking with each other. Neither one appears interested in helping you. Neither bothers to ask if you need help. You get a little annoyed by their attitudes and lack of interest. You consider asking one of them to help you, but both of their attitudes already sent a powerful message. So, you look at the computers on display, read the feature sheet for each, and make a mental note of the prices before you leave.

Attitude Action: As you enter the store, one of the cashiers greets you, "Hi, How are you today?" "Great, thanks." You mention that you're interested in a new computer and then walk to the area where they're displayed. You notice two salespeople arranging software on a shelf. Even though they're joking around, they look at you immediately. They both smile and one of them walks right over to you. *"Hi, how can I help you?"* (welcome)

Tone of Voice and Body Language Communicate Volumes

Tone of voice and body language are major components of communication. In fact, your body language is actually more important than the words you say because feelings and emotions are reflected outward and communicated through your facial expressions, gestures, and even your posture. You may say the right words, but if your tone and body language don't match, people are going to pay more attention to nonverbal cues than to the words you're voicing.

Sample Tone of Voice and Body Language Actions

Read through the following list and then analyze your tone of voice and body language when dealing with customers. Incorporate these and other actions, and you'll form good habits.

- Keep a friendly facial expression.
- Hold your head high.
- Smile, when appropriate.
- Make eye contact.
- Maintain a relaxed, open demeanor.
- Relax your shoulders.
- Maintain good posture.
- Allow gestures to flow naturally.
- Keep your hands out of your pockets.
- Try not to fidget.
- Act confidently.
- Don't chew gum or eat in the presence of customers.
- Dress for success—and check yourself in a mirror periodically throughout the day.
- Always speak in a tone of voice that sounds professional, helpful, and nonthreatening.
- Match your tone to the customer's mood, when appropriate.
- Nod from time to time to show you're listening.

Incorporating Tone of Voice and Body Language Actions

Your face can be a snapshot of your attitude and emotions. Make sure your facial expressions match what you're saying. When listening, smile, look enthusiastic, show concern, or remain passive, but match your expressions to your customer's emotions. It's important to make eye contact, but not to the point that you appear to be staring or glaring, which might make your customer uncomfortable. Maintain a relaxed and open demeanor by maintaining good posture and allowing your hands to fall naturally at your sides. Gestures should flow naturally. If they're too exaggerated, people will pay more attention to your movements than to what you're saying. Speak in a tone that's professional and projects your positive attitude. When communicating with a customer who's upset, allow your tone of voice to convey concern and compassion. If a customer is excited, match that with an enthusiastic tone. In other words, matching your tone to your conversation shows your customers that you're listening and paying attention.

Powerful Actions Make the Difference

Action: You're late for an appointment because you couldn't find a parking space. Then, as you were running into the building, you tripped on the curb and skinned your knees. As you're explaining what happened in a frustrated tone, you notice the employee is looking blankly at you, causing you to wonder if she's heard a word you said.

Tone of Voice and Body Language Action: As you're explaining your frustration in trying to find a parking space, the employee has a concerned look on her face. When you mention that you tripped on the curb, she says, "*Oh my gosh, that's awful. I have a first aid kit in my desk. Let me get you an antiseptic wipe. And don't worry about being late. I'm going to get you in as soon as I can. I'm awfully sorry all that happened to you.*" (**empathy, rapport, assurance, regret**) You can hear her concern, as well as her assurance, in the tone of her voice.

Ethical Behavior Matters

When you make a habit of always doing the right thing, your life becomes less complicated. By treating everyone equitably, you'll take and remain on the high road. When people act ethically, others trust them. When people make a habit of always telling the truth, life becomes less complicated. You don't have to remember what you said and to whom you said it. When people act unethically, others find out. When people are dishonest, the truth has a way of coming out. To keep your life less complicated, always act ethically and honestly. It's the right way to live!

Sample Ethical Actions

The importance of ethics and honesty can't be stressed enough. Besides, when you always think about your actions and do the right thing you'll feel good about yourself.

- Always act with integrity.
- Do the right thing.
- If you're not sure what the right thing is, ask for help.
- Always tell the truth.
- If you can't tell the truth, it may be better to say nothing.
- Treat others with dignity and respect.
- Be trustworthy.
- Be dependable and reliable.
- Stay accountable for your actions.
- Do what you say you will when you say you will.
- Follow through on your commitments.

Incorporating Ethical Actions

Always act in an ethical manner by choosing the right path. Think before acting. Do the right thing, and you won't have to question your conduct or second guess your decisions. Think before speaking. Always tell the truth, but if you find yourself in a sticky situation where telling the truth will be hurtful to the other person, it's probably best not to say anything. When you act ethically and honestly, you show others that you're trustworthy. By doing what you say you will when you say you will, you also show that you're dependable and reliable. Make commitments you know you can meet; it's more important to be honest with customers than to say what you think they want to hear. Always, always, follow through on your promises.

Powerful Actions Make the Difference

Action: You had a new washer and dryer installed yesterday. You were thrilled that you got the items on sale, but you just spoke to a friend who told you she bought the same appliances at the same sale price and also got the employee to throw in free delivery. You're now fuming. You're going to call the company and complain that you didn't get the same deal.

Ethical Action: When you were telling your friend how happy you were with the sale price for your washer and dryer, she commented that she was in the same store and told the employee she'd buy them if they threw in free delivery. When the employee told her they couldn't do that because they didn't offer the same deal to all their customers, she ordered the appliances anyway. After hanging up, you feel even better knowing this company values its customers enough to treat everyone the same.

Energy Level Keeps You Level Headed

Keeping your energy level steady throughout the day helps you perform consistently rather than seesawing between highs and lows. Think of your body as a valuable machine. If you don't fuel it properly, it's not going to run properly. If you don't do routine maintenance, parts are going to break down. If you don't give it a rest from time to time, it's going to peter out. Food is your body's fuel, so what you eat is important for maintaining a consistent energy level. Exercise is your body's maintenance and helps to boost your energy level by pumping oxygen through your body. Sleep is your body's rejuvenator and helps you think clearly. You can only operate at peak performance when you take full and complete care of you.

Sample Energy Actions

You'll feel so much better when you get into the habit of eating healthy foods, exercising, and getting enough rest every day.

- Eat a balanced and healthy breakfast to start your day right.
- Include whole grains, protein, fruit, vegetables, and low- or no-fat dairy products in your daily diet.
- Control fat and sugar intake.
- When you start feeling your energy level waning, refuel with healthy and nutritious choices.
- Incorporate regular exercise into your daily plan.
- If you feel drowsy, stand up, stretch, walk, or take some deep breaths to pump up your energy level.
- Get enough rest every night.
- Go to sleep around the same time so your body gets used to this schedule.

- Balance, moderation, and variety are important components in both your diet and exercise routine.

Incorporating Energy Actions

Eating well, exercising, and getting enough sleep are the key components to maintaining a consistently high energy level throughout each day. Make healthy food choices, and you'll stay satisfied longer. Thirty to sixty minutes of daily exercise is what most doctors advise. Sleep is crucial to performance, and most of us actually do need around eight hours sleep every night. When you eat well, exercise, and get the proper amount of sleep, you'll also receive important psychological benefits: a decrease in stress and tension. You'll roll with the punches easier. But remember that everyone deals with less than ideal circumstances, which can easily zap anyone's energy level. When that happens, getting away from the situation for a few minutes and giving yourself time to regroup will help. The first rule of maintaining a consistently high energy level is to be sure to take care of you everyday—not just on weekends, not just when you can fit it in.

Powerful Actions Make the Difference

Action: The sales clerk explaining the benefits of the home security system looks like he can barely keep his eyes open. He's trying hard to stifle yawns, but his eyes are drooping and he's talking so slowly and so softly you have a hard time understanding what he's saying. As he's winding down his sales pitch, you're still unclear about the system and make a joke that he should get more sleep tonight. Then you thank him and leave the store.

Energy Action: The sales clerk explaining the benefits of the home security is enthusiastic as he's telling you the benefits of the home security system. His energy and enthusiasm is so contagious you purchase the system, even though you haven't shopped around for a better price.

Calming Techniques Keep You in Control

Staying calm in the face of adversity keeps you in control. Learning calming techniques will keep you thinking sensibly and logically, will keep you from reacting or overreacting, and will keep you from spewing out words you don't mean to say and acting in ways you don't want your customers to see. Yet, there may be times when you're so upset about something you feel ready to explode. And, there may also be times when an angry or upset customer who looks ready to explode approaches you. When either of these situations occurs, use all of your self-control and inner strength to make the situation better, not worse. Put your positive attitude and high energy to good use and learn the basic habits that will help you stay calm no matter the situation.

Sample Calming Actions

Below are some of the general techniques that will help you stay calm and in control in any situation.

- Breathe slowly and deeply.
- Count to ten.
- Take a short mental break, and think about something that makes you happy.
- When someone speaks disrespectfully to you, don't take it personally.
- Listen carefully, and allow the person to vent.
- Look at the situation from the other person's perspective.

- Always think before you speak.
- Always think before you act.
- If you feel you're going to lose control of your emotions, walk away or take a time out rather than saying something you'll regret.

Incorporating Calming Actions

You're going to learn many techniques throughout this book to help you stay calm and in control of any situation. By following the basic steps above, you'll begin training yourself to form the good habit of maintaining a calm demeanor no matter the circumstance or the person. This can't be stressed enough: when you stay calm, you stay in control, and when you stay in control, you're going to handle every situation to the best of your ability. Calming techniques give you power over the situation. When you lose it, neither you nor your customer win in the end.

Powerful Actions Make the Difference

Action: You're upset with the poor service you're receiving at a restaurant. When you receive the wrong entrée, you lose it and ask to speak to the manager. As you're heatedly complaining about the service, the manager looks at you with an angry facial expression, raises her hands signaling you to back off, and says in a sarcastic tone, "Sir, I'll take care of it, but you don't have to speak to me like that." You become more upset by the manager's tone and body language and vow never to eat here again.

Calming Action: As you angrily complain about the service, you notice the manager listens carefully, takes a deep breath, and pauses a moment to formulate her response before calmly saying, *"Sir, I'm so sorry this happened."* (**courtesy, regret**) As she continues to explain that she will speak to the server, get you the correct meal right away, and also take your meal off the bill, you immediately calm down, appreciating that she kept control of her emotions and was able to quickly diffuse your anger and handle the situation appropriately.

Do This!

Jessica works in the women's department of a large clothing chain. It had been a slow morning, and she thought about calling her best friend for a brief chat. She thought the better of it, though, and knowing that was against company policy, she busied herself straightening sweaters on a display table. When she heard someone say, "Excuse me, can you help me?," she realized she had been so involved with her task she hadn't noticed the woman with a dress in her hand.

Giving the customer her full attention, Jessica said, *"Good morning! I'm sorry I didn't see you there. How are you doing today?"* (**welcome, courtesy, rapport**)

"I'm fine, thanks."

Jessica smiled and enthusiastically said, *"I'll check you out right away."* (**enthusiasm**)

"Well, actually I'd like this dress in a size eight. I haven't had any luck in finding it out here. Can you check to see if you have it?"

Jessica knew all the stock was out, but the woman looked like she really loved the dress. Instead of brushing her off, Jessica maintained eye contact and said in a helpful tone, "Our stock is all out, but *I can tell how much you like that particular dress. Let me check in the back anyway. You never know. I'll also check the dressing rooms. Sometimes people leave clothes in them. I'll be right back."* (**assurance, empathy, courtesy**) Her energy level and eagerness to help made the customer feel confident that Jessica would do all she could to find the dress.

When she came back, she said apologetically, *"Thanks for waiting. I'm sorry, I couldn't find it. Let me do one more thing, though.* I'm going to check and see if any of our other stores have it. If they do *I'll be happy to order it* and we can have it sent here for you to pick up." **(courtesy, regret, assurance, enthusiasm)**

"Would you? That would be great, thanks so much."

Jessica finished the transaction by ordering the correct size from another store. *"I'm so glad I could find the dress for you. Thanks for coming in today."* **(appreciation)**

"Thank you! I'm glad I came in too."

Why This Works

Throughout this contact, Jessica's actions mirrored her words. She showed that she was an ethical employee by doing the right thing and not phoning her friend even though she was bored at work. Instead, she found busy work to do and, although she hadn't been paying attention when the customer was waiting, it didn't matter to the customer because as soon as Jessica noticed her, she paid complete attention and listened fully. She projected a great attitude by staying interested in finding the best solution for the customer. She displayed her positive attitude through her tone of voice and body language. Her smile and eye contact conveyed her high-energy level. When she couldn't find the dress, Jessica did the right thing by offering to order the dress from another store to the obvious delight of her customer.

PART II

Powerful Phrases and Scripts for Every Situation

3

Powerful Phrases for Typical Customer Interactions

When you incorporate powerful phrases into your customer interactions and back up your words with appropriate actions, you put yourself in position to handle all customers to their satisfaction. In every contact, it's important to get the customer on your side. And that should be easy, at least with those customers who are easy to deal with and easy to satisfy.

Chapters 4 and 5 get to the heart of this book: you will learn how to handle all those less than ideal situations that make working in the customer service field so tough. Right now, though, let's focus on those customer situations that are typical. Hopefully, the majority of your customers have a good idea of what they want, listen to your proposed solutions, are courteous and respectful toward you, work with you to find an agreeable solution, and are satisfied at the end of the transaction.

By combining your words, phrases, and actions into a six-step process, you'll achieve the goal of finding the best solution for each customer quickly, correctly, and with a great attitude. In ideal customer interactions, the customer is on your side throughout the interaction, so following the process should be straightforward. And, as you'll learn in the following chapters, when your customers aren't easy to deal with, don't have an idea of what they want, aren't always courteous and respectful, you'll be able to pinpoint at which step the interaction headed south, regroup, go back to that step, rework it, and complete the interaction successfully.

You may not have thought about dealing with customers as a step-by-step process, but it's really that simple. In every customer contact, three distinct phases can be identified that must be completed for a successful outcome: an introduction phase (meet and greet), a helping phase (understand and assist), and a concluding phase (agree and acknowledge). These three phases are broken down into the six-step process. When you follow the steps and choose powerful phrases and actions, you'll create a dialogue that's going to work in any customer interaction: from those that are ideal to those that are miles from that.

Remember that even when your customers aren't right, even when they behave badly, it's their perceptions of good service that matter. You'll only satisfy them when they feel that you treated them well. Follow the six-step process, and you'll receive rave reviews every time you're in the act.

MEET AND GREET

In this phase, you set the stage for the entire interaction with your customer. In less than ten seconds after they enter, they'll pay attention to all aspects of your appearance, such as your clothing, grooming, posture, and overall demeanor. Even in those instances in which your customers don't begin forming a positive impression of you (and in some cases this will happen no matter how well you're dressed, groomed, and carry yourself), you can turn around a customer's poor impression by offering a heartfelt greeting. When you make a good impression and greet each customer with enthusiasm, you greatly enhance your chances for a successful second and third act.

STEP 1: MAKE A GREAT FIRST IMPRESSION

The reason making a great first impression comes before greeting customers is that first impressions are so important, they can instantly enhance or detract from your ability to successfully interact with customers. The moment customers see you, they begin forming their impressions—in fact, we all do this when we encounter others. Sometimes we don't know why, but we form a poor first impression based on our subjective views about people who are different from us. And sometimes we can't even pinpoint why.

The same can happen when others are forming their impression of you. Maintaining an appearance appropriate to the work you do and presenting a pleasant demeanor increases your chances of having customers form positive opinions of you. Customers pay attention to your physical appearance: your hair, nails, grooming, clothes, and shoes. They also notice your demeanor: your facial expressions, posture, and gestures. When you are well groomed, dressed appropriately for the work you do, and nothing about you looks out of place, customers are likely to begin forming a positive first impression. When you make eye contact and smile, and when your posture and gestures send a positive signal, customers are likely to view you favorably.

When you interact with customers by phone or online, you can make a great first impression through your tone of voice and the manner in which you write. Smile when you speak. Reflect your personality when you speak or write. Always project a positive attitude and an eagerness to help.

The most important rule to remember is that you should always be mindful to look your best and present yourself so that others will likely form a good first impression. After all, you never know who it is you're impressing. You might impress a customer who turns out to be the owner of your company . . . or a relative of the person you're dating . . . or the job interviewer you have an appointment with . . . or the person whom you later call upon to help you with something. You just never know!

Sample First Impression Behaviors

Customers are likely to form a favorable first impression of you when you do the following:

- Pay attention to your physical appearance, cleanliness, and grooming: Be sure that your clothes are clean, pressed, and appropriate to your environment, your shoes are in good repair, your hair is combed and styled, and your nails are neatly trimmed and clean.
- Always dress professionally. When you look professional you'll act more professional.
- If you work in a casual environment, you can still look professional by making sure your clothes are clean and neat looking. No holey tees or ripped, shredded jeans!
- Pay attention to your body language: Be sure that your facial expressions convey friendliness, interest, enthusiasm, or concern, as appropriate to the situation. Maintain good posture, gesture smoothly, and stand so that your arms are relaxed by your sides or your hands are folded in front of you.
- Make eye contact and smile.
- Always project a positive attitude and a desire to help.

- When making a first impression on the phone or through email, smile when you speak and reflect your personality when you write.
- Periodically perform a quick check to make sure you're maintaining good posture and that your facial expressions are pleasant.
- Ask someone you trust to tell you when something's amiss.

Do This!

Joe is sales rep in a cell phone store. His customer service job duties include greeting customers, guiding them to check in on the computer terminals, and handling their requests in a timely manner. Today, when he took a bite of his sandwich at lunch, mustard spurted out and stained his white shirt. When Joe arrived back at the store for his afternoon shift, he was embarrassed by the visible yellow stain on his shirt. He called the next customer in line, and as the woman approached him, he noticed that she was looking at the stain rather than at him. With an exaggerated hand gesture, he covered it up, looked sheepishly at the customer, and then smiled. The customer laughed and nodded amusedly.

Why This Works

Joe understood that the stain on his shirt could draw unfavorable attention to his appearance. By putting a humorous spin on his situation, Joe hoped that the customer wouldn't form a negative opinion of him. This diffused any negative thoughts the customer may have had about Joe's appearance. Rather than forming a negative impression, the customer got the impression that he cared about his appearance, was otherwise well groomed, and was embarrassed by the stain on his shirt.

Step 2: Greet the Customer

Your greeting, including a phrase of welcome, can enhance the positive impression customers are forming. But let's say that something about your appearance doesn't look right—just like Joe. You know that customers are going to pay more attention to what's amiss than what's right and that can cause them to form an unfavorable first impression. Your greeting, in these situations, can turn a negative first impression into a positive one. Choosing the right words, using good grammar, enunciating clearly, and speaking courteously communicate to your customers that you have a positive attitude and are willing to help.

Your company may have a standard greeting for you to use and, if that's the case, say it enthusiastically. Say it like you're happy the customer chose your business. Say it like you're eager to help. If your company doesn't have a standard greeting, you can create your own, including a welcome message that conveys your desire to be of assistance.

Speaking with enthusiasm indicates your eagerness to help, but if you've picked up a clue about attitude from your customer's facial expression and demeanor, it's best to try to match your tone to his or her emotions. For example, if a customer looks as though she's upset about something, offer a greeting with concern in your voice. If a customer appears angry, greet him by speaking calmly and controlling your voice inflection.

When you present yourself in a manner in which customers form a favorable impression and when you incorporate phrases of welcome in your greeting, you'll begin to establish a rapport with them. Find common ground and show that you're friendly, trustworthy, considerate, and interested in each customer.

Sample Greeting Behaviors

Rather than relying on the hope that your customers are forming a positive first impression and that they're on your side when you begin your interaction, complete Act 1 by doing the following:

- Stop whatever you're doing and pay attention when a customer comes in.

- Answer the phone on the first ring.

- Respond to emails or Internet requests promptly.

- Add powerful phrases of welcome to your greetings.

- Greet every customer with a tone of voice that conveys interest and eagerness to help.

- Smile, make eye contact, choose the right words, use good grammar, and enunciate clearly.

- Give your name when appropriate.

- Include in your welcome message a statement or question conveying your desire to help.

- Use the customer's name if you know it.

- Begin building rapport by finding common ground.

Do This!

Joe greeted the customer by saying, *"Good afternoon! You'll have to excuse the way I look. I enjoyed my lunch so much I wanted to bring some of it back to work with me."* (**welcome, regret, rapport**)

The customer laughed with him and said, "I've done that myself!"

"My name is Joe. How are you doing?" (**welcome, rapport**)

"I'm doing great, thank you. How are you?"

"I'm doing great too, *thanks. How can I help you today?*" Joe asked enthusiastically. **(courtesy, welcome)**

Why This Works

When Joe greeted the customer he felt it was important to immediately begin building a rapport, which could help the customer complete forming her positive first impression, so he humorously explained why his shirt was stained. This diffused any negative thoughts the customer may have been having about him. When he completed his powerful words of welcome by asking how he could help, the customer felt she was in good hands.

UNDERSTAND AND ASSIST

You made a great first impression. You greeted your customer and asked how you could help. Congratulations! Unless this is a difficult customer contact, you already have the customer on your side. And you've set yourself up to handle the rest of the interaction successfully. The beginning and end of the contact are usually pretty typical: you meet and greet, and you agree on the proposed solution and acknowledge your customers' decisions by showing appreciation to them. Between the beginning and the end is the meat of the interaction. This part can be as short as showing a customer where to find a product or it can be as involved as answering questions, providing detailed information, and then assisting the customer by researching a solution. The middle phase is where you're going to meet the customer service goal of finding the best solution for each customer.

Step 3: Understand the Customer's Request

You know that the only way to give truly great service is to first understand what the customer wants. That's the key. It's that simple: How will you find the best solution when you don't know what solution you're looking for? It's not going to happen! Okay, maybe it will some of the time. Think of it as taking an exam you haven't studied for and marking random answers. The law of logics suggests that you'll get some of the answers correct. But with customers do you want to take the chance to get it correct some of the time? Not if you want to keep your job. Satisfy each customer and you improve your chances that they'll come back. That's job security!

Sample Understanding the Request Behaviors

Before you can find the best solution for each customer, you'll need to do the following to ensure you understand correctly:

- Pay attention. You're heard this before, and you're going to hear it again. It's that important.
- Listen to the customer's opening statement. Never make a customer repeat because you weren't paying attention. Doing so may reverse the positive impression your customer has been forming of you.
- Summarize the opening statement if you feel it'll help and any time you're not sure you understood correctly.
- Assure the customer that you're going to help, whether it's a simple question or an interaction that's going to take a while.
- Listen completely throughout the interaction. Shut out distractions.
- When listening, remain objective; don't judge or presume you know what the customer wants. And don't finish their sentences. Allow the customer to get it all out.

- Pay attention to the customer's body language to pick up any non-verbal clues.
- Ask good questions to complete your understanding. Use a combination of open questions (to gather information) and closed questions (to clarify information).
- After you finished asking questions, summarize the customer's needs to make sure you really do understand.
- If your customer is face to face with you, show and tell. Showing and telling helps you gain a better understanding of your customer's needs because you can pick up on cues.
- If it's a lengthy contact, take notes. You might think you'll remember everything, but why take the chance?

Do This!

"I'm looking for a new cell phone. I'm pretty sure my contract is up on my old phone and, if it is, I'd like to get a smart phone."

"*I'll be happy to help you with that.*" Joe smiled warmly. "Let's start by getting your account number, *please.*" (**enthusiasm, courtesy**)

After the customer gave her number, Joe pulled up her account on his computer screen, then said, "*Absolutely* correct, *Ms. Carpenter*! You're contract was up last month so you're eligible for a new phone. When you upgrade to a smart phone, in addition to the one-time charge for the phone, there's also a monthly increase of around thirty dollars." (**enthusiasm, courtesy**)

She nodded, and then he asked, "Do you have a particular phone in mind?"

It was the customer's turn to look sheepish. "No, I'm afraid I don't know much about them. All my friends are getting them, so I figured it's time I get one too."

"No problem. *I'll be happy to help*. Since you don't know which one you want, I'll show you each of the ones we have and explain how they work." **(enthusiasm)**

Joe patiently walked the customer to each of the phone displays, giving a quick tutorial and explaining the pros and cons of each model. When he was done, he noticed that she looked baffled, so he said, "*I know it can be a little overwhelming*. What apps do you think you'll use the most?" **(empathy)**

"Well, I guess I'd download music and a news app for sure, and then probably some games. Beyond that, I'll have to figure it out. I travel frequently for my job, so I can see myself using the apps during down time at airports, but as I said, I really don't know that much about these phones."

"*Thanks. That helps me a lot. It sounds like the most important factors are that you want a smart phone that will be easy to learn and easy to use.*" **(courtesy, rapport)**

"You got it!"

"Now what about the one-time cost for the phone? As I explained when I was showing them to you, there's a range of prices."

"Not the most important factor. I'd rather get a phone I'll be able to learn easily and get the most enjoyment out of."

Why This Works

Because Joe paid attention and listened completely throughout this phase of the contact, he developed a good understanding of both the customer's needs and her comfort level with using the phones. He asked good questions to determine her needs and discovered how she thought she'd use her phone. His enthusiasm and interest in finding the best solution helped Ms. Carpenter develop trust in Joe, and as he performed his "show and tell," he also demonstrated that he was competent and understood the products he was offering. She felt confident that he had her best interests in mind. By summarizing her needs, including the cost which could be a determining factor in this scenario, he ensured that he understood exactly what she was looking for.

Step 4: Assist the Customer

Once you understand what your customers want, it's your job to match the best solution to their needs. You might discover the solution immediately, or you might have to do some research and make a commitment to get back to him or her. The most important factor in this step is that you take the necessary time to find the best solution. It means fully understanding your customer's needs and matching the solution, efficiently, and effectively.

Sample Finding the Best Solution Behaviors

When it comes to assisting your customers and finding the best solution for each, they depend on you to do the right thing. They consider you to be the expert, so:

- When finding the best solution, find it as quickly as possible.
- Always do the right thing for your customer, even if it means you don't get a sale or won't make a commission on the transaction.
- Don't make hasty decisions unless the best solution jumps out at you. Consider the information you gathered from the customer and base your decisions on individual needs.
- Never trade efficiency for effectiveness. It's always best to take a little more time to do what's best for each customer.

- Base your recommendation on what the customer told you.

- When you've found the best solution, fully explain your proposal.

- When making your proposal, refer to key points the customer mentioned.

- Offer your best solution first. This isn't the time to offer a mediocre solution and play *Let's Make a Deal.*.

- Explain your reasons for offering this solution.

- Focus on what you can do, rather than on what you can't do.

- If you're resolving a problem and feel it's important to maintain the integrity of your proposal, explain what happened and why it happened, and then offer your solution.

- When you're figuring out the best solution and have to place your customer on phone hold or pause the conversation, explain what you're doing.

- Handle email or online inquiries with the same diligence you would answer a question from a customer standing in front of you.

Do This!

"Great. Let's go back to the last one I showed you," Joe suggested. "It isn't the cheapest, *but as you said, that's not the most important factor in your decision."* (**enthusiasm, rapport**)

Ms Carpenter nodded and followed Joe back to the display. "This one is considered the gold standard of smart phones," he explained. He reviewed the features of the phone again and then confidently stated, "From everything you've told me, this is the phone I'd recommend. You mentioned your learning curve, and *I can certainly understand that. This is the easiest one to learn and the easiest one to navigate."* (**empathy, rapport**)

Why This Works

Throughout this step, Joe referred to key points his customer had mentioned were important to her. Joe explained that he wasn't showing her the cheapest phone, but rather the model that was the easiest to use. By referring to her own words, he showed that he had paid attention to her, listened closely, identified her needs, and was confident that he found the best solution for her.

AGREE AND ACKNOWLEDGE

You asked good questions and made sure you understood the customer's request. You found what you consider the best solution for your customer, and you presented your proposal. Depending on the nature of your job, the first parts of your interaction may have taken a few minutes, several hours, or even days. Regardless, by first making sure you fully understood the customer's request, you put yourself in a great position to find the right solution. Once you offer your solution, the last two steps ensure the customer agrees with your proposal. When he or she signals positively, end the contact by acknowledging the customer's decision and showing appreciation.

Step 5: Gain Agreement

You made your proposal. Great. Now what? Before ending the contact, you need to make sure the customer likes your solution. If you fully understood the request and if you fully understand your company's products and services, your proposal should be on point. Now it's time to wind down the contact, so to speak, to make sure the customer is in sync with your proposed solution. If he or she is, that makes the rest of the contact simple and straightforward. There will be times, though, when your customer isn't in agreement, and you'll have to regroup and rework your solution. When your customer hesitates, has questions, objects, or outright refuses your proposed solution, you need to take a couple steps back and ask more questions to clarify why he or she doesn't agree. Perhaps you didn't understand correctly. Perhaps the customer doesn't like what you offered. Perhaps it's a money issue. By asking more questions, you'll be able to clear up misunderstandings and find a solution that's agreeable to your customer.

Sample Gaining Agreement Behaviors

Gaining agreement is the only way to truly gauge customer satisfaction. The following will help you do that:

- After offering your proposed solution, ask a question to make sure your customer understands.
- Then, ask if the customer accepts your proposal.
- If the customer agrees to your proposed solution, acknowledge the agreement.
- Recap your proposal so the customer knows exactly what you'll do.
- If the customer doesn't agree to your proposed solution, go back to Step 3 and ask qualifying questions to clear up any misunderstandings.
- Pay attention to body language to gauge the customer's emotions.
- If you still feel your original proposal is the best solution, explain why you feel that way.
- If you find another solution based on the additional information the customer provided, offer that and again ask for agreement.

- Never try to shove your solution down a customer's throat! Sometimes it's best to agree to disagree, especially when a customer is insistent on the outcome.

- When you're involved in a situation in which the customer insists on a solution that you don't agree with, it's okay to state your reasoning again to make sure he or she understands your point of view, but then go with what the customer wants.

- If you can't find a workable solution but need to, ask the customer for his or her suggestions on a solution and, if it's a viable option, agree to it.

- In the event that you can't find the best solution, ask your manager for help.

Do This!

Joe then asked, "What do you think?"

He noticed Ms. Carpenter still looked a little confused. When she didn't immediately acknowledge, he said, "*You look a little unsure. What questions do you have?*" (**empathy, rapport**)

"None, really. You did a good job explaining all the phones, and I'm leaning toward getting this one. I'm just not sure I'm going to figure it all out."

"*This is the one I have, and I really like it. In fact, I got one for my mother, who knew nothing about smart phones, and she caught on quickly. You won't have any trouble using this phone and once you start downloading apps, you'll find that you're going to get a lot of use out of it. After I set it up, I'll show you how to download a few apps I think you'll like. Then, if you ever have a question or a problem, you can always come in or call. We'll be happy to help with anything.*" (**rapport, enthusiasm**)

With that, she smiled and said, "Okay. You sold me. I trust your judgment, and I'll take it."

"*Great!* To recap, we're going to upgrade your service to this phone. I'll need to complete some paperwork, and I'll explain all the charges. I'll show you how to download apps, and you'll be good to go. *I guarantee you'll like this phone, especially during those long waits you have at airports!*" **(enthusiasm, rapport)**

Why This Works

When Joe asked if his proposal was agreeable, he paid attention to the customer's body language and picked up on her hesitancy to make a buying decision. He quickly responded by asking what questions she had. Because he believed this was the best solution for her, rather than possibly adding to her confusion by showing her other models, he restated why he felt this was best for her. After gaining her agreement, he recapped and explained what he was going to do.

Step 6: Acknowledge the Customer

Whether you were able to find a workable solution or your customer decides not to accept your proposal, always end your interactions by acknowledging and accepting the customer's decision. This is a simple step, often quickly handled in one question or statement, yet it's extremely important because it's the last, and lasting, impression you leave with your customers. When you take a moment to acknowledge them, whether or not they do business with you, you send a powerful, positive message that you value your customers and that they're all important to you.

Sample Acknowledgment Behaviors

Acknowledge and show appreciation to every customer by doing the following:

- After agreeing on the solution, validate the customer's decision, whether or not it was your suggestion, and even if he or she hasn't agreed to any solution. (In other words, if the customer leaves without buying or deciding).

- If the customer agreed with your solution, a simple *I'm sure you'll enjoy your* . . . acknowledges your confidence in the decision.

- If the customer didn't agree with your solution, a simple phrase of regret such as, *I'm sorry I couldn't help you today* . . . acknowledges your respect for the customer's decision.

- After offering an acknowledgment, ask the customer if you can help with anything else.

- Finish your contact with a heartfelt phrase of appreciation.

- Repeat your name and offer to help in the future if you feel it pertinent to your interaction.

Do This!

After Joe completed the contract and Ms. Carpenter signed it, he handed her a copy along with a bag containing the accessories she chose. He then gave her a quick tutorial and showed her how to download apps, as well as downloaded some free ones he thought she'd like.

Then he said, "*I know you're going to like your new phone. Is there anything else I can help you with?*" (**rapport, appreciation**)

She was visibly excited. "Thank you so much for all your help. Now that you showed me how to use it, I know I'll love it."

"*Terrific! Ms. Carpenter, thank you so much for coming in today.*

We appreciate your loyalty as our customer." (**enthusiasm, courtesy, appreciation**)

"I'm so glad I came in too. Thank you."

Why This Works

After gaining agreement, Joe acknowledged and validated the customer's decision by saying he knew she'd like her new phone. By asking if he could help with anything else, he gave Ms. Carpenter the opportunity to pause and think for a moment in case she had any questions. When she didn't, he thanked her for her business, and added an appreciation statement telling her that his company appreciated her loyalty. This simple statement showed that he and his company valued her as their customer.

4

Powerful Phrases for Challenging Customer Behaviors

Customers aren't one size fits all. They're not even one size fits most. Rather, they come in all shapes, sizes, and ... personalities. What about those customers who are challenging to handle? How do you handle those out of the ordinary customers—those who push your buttons—without becoming unwound, upset, or unglued? In this chapter, you're going to learn how to handle many different types of personalities and quirks, warts and all. You'll learn how to overcome bad customer behaviors, get the customer on your side, and move through the steps to provide the best solution quickly and correctly, while maintaining a positive attitude.

As a frontline employee responsible for handling customers, you've already dealt with those who behave badly, who leave you scrambling for the right words to say or the right actions to take. In these situations, you've got to remind yourself that you can't control how someone treats you; you can only control how you react to that person's behavior. You're in charge of you, so staying calm and cool is the solution to handling any customer with confidence, control, and poise. Remember: Don't take anyone's bad behavior personally!

Learning how to quickly identify the difficult behavior or personality type is the first step in knowing how best to handle the customer and the situation. The second step is learning how to quickly regroup, deal with the behavior, and redirect the conversation so that you maintain control. When you do that you can pick up where you left off in the six steps of successful customer interactions (see chapter 3, pages **00-00**) and move the interaction forward to a positive outcome. For example, if you greet the customer and ask how you can help and the customer immediately yells at you, you'll identify the behavior type as anger, quickly deal with that behavior by speaking and acting in a way that gets the customer on your side, and then pick up the next step to begin building a rapport.

In this chapter, many different behaviors are described. Each behavior and appropriate approach is identified with examples, along with a *Do This!* scenario with an appropriate dialog. You'll learn how to apply each approach to your particular work environment and your customer interactions. As in the first three chapters, the powerful phrases are denoted in *italics* with the type powerful phrase noted in (**bold**). For some of the behaviors, a "Quick Tip for a Sticky Situation" is included as well, demonstrating how to handle a situation that can be particularly difficult.

What to Do When the Customer Is Agitated

Agitation often shows up when something takes longer than the customer expected. It can indicate someone who has a tough time dealing with stress and is about to lose control; a Type-A personality, which refers to people who are highly emotional, excitable, impatient, and aggressive; or it can sometimes be a symptom of people with dementia or Alzheimer's, a condition in which the person no longer has the mental capacity to act in a reasonable manner and becomes overwrought, often with no provocation.

When you encounter a customer who is agitated, you should be able to identify the behavior fairly quickly. If you're working with a customer who has been calm but displays increasing signs of agitation, consider that this person may feel you're taking too long handling the request, is in a hurry to get someplace else, is stressed, or is a Type-A personality. Signs of dementia can usually be identified during your conversation, as you begin to notice a problem communicating with the person. No matter what the reason is, speaking in a calm, soft, caring voice should improve the customer's behavior. Your main goal is to lessen the feelings of agitation. If you have suspicions that the customer may be disturbed due to dementia, it's never all right to make fun of the customer or act in a disrespectful manner.

Identifying the Behavior

An agitated customer may:

- Act jumpy.
- Appear nervous.
- Shift gaze from one spot to another continually.

- Fidget with keys or change in pocket.
- Look at watch frequently.
- Play with hair.
- Drum fingers noisily.
- Display jerky behaviors, such as shifting from foot to foot, or when seated, tapping a foot.
- Change demeanor without warning.
- Quickly go from perturbed to disturbed.

Do This!

Elizabeth works for an insurance agency. She's handling a walk-in customer who's concerned that she doesn't have adequate homeowner's coverage. The customer recently moved to the East Coast and with hurricane season beginning, she asked Elizabeth to review her policy.

Employee: *"I'm glad you came in today. My name is Elizabeth, and I'll be happy to review your policy, Mrs. Matthews. Please have a seat and I'll pull your policy up on my screen. Hurricane season gets us all thinking, doesn't it?"* **(welcome, enthusiasm, courtesy, rapport)**

Agitated Customer: "Yes, it sure does. When I saw on the news this morning that hurricane season starts tomorrow, I thought I'd better have someone look over my coverage. I don't want to appear paranoid but I had a little time before I need to get to work, so I figured I'd come in."

Employee: *"You're not paranoid at all. I certainly understand your feelings. Always better to be safe than sorry. I have your policy on my screen. Let me read through it and if I see anything that needs to be added or changed, I'll get it taken care of right away for you."* **(rapport, empathy, assurance)**

> (As Elizabeth was reading through the policy, she noticed the customer looked at her watch and then began drum-

ming her fingers on the desk. Elizabeth identified that the customer was becoming agitated and assumed it was because she mentioned she had to get to work. Perhaps she was concerned that she'd be late.)

Employee: "*You mentioned that you stopped in before you need to get to work.* I'm about halfway through reviewing your policy. Do you have the time now for me to continue?" **(rapport)**

Customer: "I didn't think it would take this long. I need to be at work by ten."

Employee: "*Oh, I understand. I don't want you to be late.* Here's what I can do. *I'll be happy to schedule a follow-up time so we can discuss the policy.* I'd rather do that than rush through it now and perhaps miss something. *Is that alright with you, Mrs. Matthews?*" **(empathy, rapport, enthusiasm, courtesy)**

Customer: "Yes, that would be great, thank you so much. I'm sorry. I guess I wasn't thinking how much time it would take."

(Elizabeth observed that the customer took a deep breath and appeared to calm down.)

Employee: "*No need to apologize. I'll thoroughly review your policy,* and I can call you this afternoon, say around two. *How does that sound?*" **(courtesy, assurance, enthusiasm)**

Customer: "Great. Thank you so much."

Employee: "*Thank you for coming in. I appreciate the opportunity to help you, and I'll call you around two this afternoon.*" **(appreciation, assurance)**

Why This Works

This worked because the employee recognized that the customer was becoming agitated and dealt with the behavior immediately, rather than continuing to read through the policy, which surely would have increased the agitation. From the beginning of the contact, Elizabeth began building a rapport. When she echoed Mrs. Matthews's comment about stopping on her way to work, she demonstrated that she was paying attention. She was empathetic toward Mrs. Matthews and, when she offered an alternative solution, Mrs. Matthews immediately calmed down. Elizabeth's attitude, tone of voice, and body language enhanced her powerful phrases and, by ending the conversation with a phrase of appreciation, the customer felt valued.

Applying the Approach

When dealing with an agitated customer, apply the following principles to your situations:

- You'll most likely encounter an agitated customer during the Meet-and-Greet phase or the Understand-and-Assist phase of your interactions. Hopefully, by the time you're in the last phase of your interaction, you've handled your customer well and he or she won't have any cause to be agitated.

- Agitation almost always shows up in visible facial expressions or body language cues, such as those previously mentioned.

- When speaking to a customer by phone, signs of agitation may be heard: loud sighing, fidgeting sounds, or drumming noises. The person may even vocalize the agitation, as in: "How long is this going to take?"

- As soon as you notice that a customer is displaying one or more of the agitation behaviors, deal with that behavior and calm the customer down.

- If you don't know why the customer is agitated, offer a phrase of empathy or assurance: *"I understand this might seem as though it's taking a long time,* or *I'm taking care of this as quickly as I can for you."*

- Offering a phrase of empathy or assurance should encourage the customer to state the reason for the agitation: "I have an appointment I need to get to."

- Resume where you left off in the six steps only when you feel that the customer is no longer agitated. Continuing the contact without calming the customer will only cause further agitation and possibly exaggerated behaviors or a worsening attitude.

- If you've established a rapport with the customer, you may feel comfortable enough to identify the specific behavior and then offer phrases of rapport and assurance: *"I noticed that you're looking at your watch. It's going to take me about ten more minutes to complete the request. Is that alright?"*

- When you're working to diffuse the agitation, show concern in your facial expressions.

- Speak in a calm, self-assured, respectful tone of voice.

What to Do When the Customer Is Angry

When a customer displays anger, he or she is usually doing so because of a mistake—or possibly a series of mistakes—made by your company. Sometimes, usually calm people become angry when mistakes keep happening. The proverbial straw breaks the camel's back, and they blow their cool. And, then there's Type-A people, who have very short fuses and are prone to angry outbursts (not to mention an increased risk of heart attacks). The bottom line is that you'll know when a customer is angry. Besides seeing the facial expressions that signal anger, customers who are angry are going to voice their feelings.

When you're dealing with an angry customer, you have to diffuse the anger before you can work through the interaction. Anger can rub off, too, because when someone speaks angrily to you, your first instinct may be to become defensive and speak in the same tone of voice. That never helps! Keep your cool and you'll stay in control of the situation.

When a customer is angry, take the bull by the horns and offer a phrase of regret. Even if you didn't do anything wrong, apologize. Even if you think the customer is out of line for directing his or her anger at you, apologize. If you have a hard time apologizing for something you didn't do, say: *"I'm sorry that happened."* You're offering a phrase of regret without accepting blame. After you apologize, immediately offer a phrase of assurance, such as *"I'm going to handle this immediately,"* and say it in a confident, self-assured tone. Usually, those two phrases, voiced with concern and confidence, will calm the customer and you can begin dealing with the problem and finding a satisfactory solution.

Identifying the Behavior

An angry person may:
- Say something that clearly identifies the behavior.
- Show anger through facial expressions: pursed lips, red faced, narrowed eyes, furrowed brow.
- Communicate in a tone that signals anger: loud voice, enunciated words, controlled monotone speech, speaking through clenched teeth.
- Shout or scream at you.
- Immediately demand a supervisor.
- Call you names.
- Speak ill of your company.
- Threaten to go somewhere else.

Do This!

Richard is a customer service rep for an appliance repair company. He took a call and, after he offered his company's standard greeting, the customer immediately began to yell at him.

Angry Customer: "This is Roy Anthony. I'm so mad I could spit bullets. You were supposed to have a repair person out this morning to fix my ice maker and no one's showed."

Employee: *"I'm so sorry, Mr. Anthony. I'll check with my dispatcher to see what happened and how soon we can get someone out. My name is Richard. May I have your phone number, please?"* **(regret, courtesy, assurance, welcome, courtesy)**

Customer: "It's 555-7634. You better get someone out right away. I'm not going to sit around all afternoon."

Employee: *"I certainly understand how you feel, Mr. Anthony. I'd be upset, too, if I waited all morning. That isn't acceptable service and certainly doesn't meet our company expectations."* **(courtesy, empathy, rapport, assurance)**

Customer: "Well, yeah, I mean, I sat here getting more and more upset as the clock ticked closer to noon. I don't mean to take it out on you. It isn't your fault, but this happened with another service company, which is why I switched to you. Now it's happened with your company, and I'm not at all happy. You made a promise you didn't keep."

Employee: *"I feel really bad that we disappointed you. We strive to meet all our commitments. I'm going to check with my dispatcher right now and get this taken care of for you. May I put you on hold while I check?"* **(empathy, assurance, courtesy)**

Customer: "Yes, I'll hold."

Employee: *"Mr. Anthony, thank you for holding.* Here's what happened. The repairman was on his way to your home when he got into an accident with someone who ran a red light. Our dispatch department has been working hard trying to get all of his jobs reassigned, and they scheduled you for this afternoon. *We should have called you to let you know what happened, and I apologize that we didn't. I've asked my dispatcher to move you to the next appointment because we inconvenienced you. A service person will be at your home no later than two this afternoon. Would that be all right?"* **(courtesy, regret, rapport, assurance)**

Customer: "Yes, that'll be fine. Gee, I'm sorry I was so upset. Is the man okay?"

Employee: *"Thanks for asking,* he's fine. The van he was driving didn't fare so well, though. *Mr. Anthony, we really appreciate your business and regret this happened. Thanks for being so understanding."* **(courtesy, appreciation, regret, appreciation)**

Customer: "Thank you, Richard."

(Later that afternoon, Richard followed up with Mr. Anthony.)

Employee: *"Mr. Anthony, this is Richard calling back. I wanted to make sure the repair person fixed your icemaker."* **(courtesy, welcome, assurance)**

Customer: "Yes, he did. Hey, thanks for calling me to check on it."

Employee: *"You're welcome, and we really appreciate your business. Again, what happened this morning doesn't normally happen* *and we hope you'll give us another chance next time you need service."* **(courtesy, appreciation, assurance)**

Customer: "I sure will, thanks again for calling."

Why This Works

From the moment Richard heard the customer's angry outburst, he knew he immediately needed to diffuse the anger before he would be able to help Mr. Anthony. The first words out of his mouth were a phrase of regret, followed by a phrase of assurance. When Richard determined Mr. Anthony hadn't calmed down, he followed up with a phrase of empathy and one of rapport. Often, letting the person know you understand and you wouldn't like it if that situation happened to you will calm down an angry customer.

However, in this scenario, the customer still wanted to vent. Rather than try to move forward to the step of assisting the customer, Richard offered additional phrases of empathy and assurance and then explained what he was going to do and asked permission to place the customer on hold. When Richard returned to the line, he explained what happened and took full responsibility for the company error by stating, *we should have called,* rather than blaming another department or employee. Throughout the conversation, he offered phrases of assurance and his attentiveness, positive attitude, and confident tone enhanced his powerful phrases. Finally, when he followed up to ensure Mr. Anthony was satisfied with the outcome, Richard made a good and lasting impression in the customer's mind.

Quick Tip for a Sticky Situation

Sometimes, customers just like to carp and complain. If you're at the point in the conversation at which you've offered your phrases of regret, assurance, empathy, and rapport and the customer still wants to vent, don't get caught in a circle of offering more of the same and then listening to more complaining. Try to tactfully move the conversation forward, as Richard did. Getting to the assisting stage is your goal, so say to a continual complainer, *"Ms. Customer, I completely understand your frustration and believe me, I'd feel the same way. I don't want to cut you off but I need to the bottom of this, find out what happened, and make it right for you. Is that agreeable to you?"* Then, if the customer still wants to complain, resign yourself to being in for the long haul of listening and empathizing. If it goes on and on, you'll want to get your supervisor involved.

Applying the Approach

When interacting with a customer who is angry, apply the following principles to your situations:

- Phrases of regret, empathy, and assurance are your keys to diffusing an angry customer.

- Immediately offer a phrase of regret: *"I'm sorry."* An apology should always be the first words out of your mouth.

- Then immediately offer a phrase of assurance: *"I'll take care of this right away."*

- Before you attempt to handle the customer, allow the customer to vent and explain why he or she is so upset to ensure you understand correctly and completely.

- After allowing the customer to vent, offer phrases of empathy and assurance: *"I can certainly understand how you feel. Now that you explained what happened I'm going to check with another department. Would you mind holding? It shouldn't take but a minute or so."*

- When you speak to an angry customer, use a confident, controlled voice tone. Be assertive and show the customer through your attentiveness and attitude that you're going to handle the problem.

- Make eye contact and keep your facial expressions passive. You don't want to mimic the customer's anger nor do you want to appear flustered or suggest by your actions that you don't know what to say or do. You know what to say and do!

- Assume your customer has a valid reason to be angry. Remember what you learned about customer perceptions: it's the customer's perception of service that matters and, when someone complains, it means in that customer's eyes, service expectations weren't met.

- Look for signals that the customer is calmed down. These are expressed either through body language and facial expressions or through the customer's response to you. Then continue to the step of assisting the customer. If you attempt to handle the problem while the customer is still angry, your efforts will not be well received.

What to Do When the Customer Is Combative

When a person allows anger, frustration, or fear to move out of control, he or she may become combative. When someone becomes combative, it's usually a means of self-protection acted out in an overly aggressive manner. Combative behavior is displayed verbally by arguing, yelling, or becoming belligerent, or physically by gesturing wildly, flailing, or lashing out at another person. An angry or frustrated customer may verbally attack an employee. A person who panics may physically lash out. Combative behavior, though often encountered in the health-care profession, may occur in any environment in which an individual feels an overwhelming sense of fear or panic as part of the need to protect himself or herself.

When you pay close attention to a customer who's angry, you'll quickly observe if he or she begins acting out, either physically or verbally. If you see any sign of aggressive, combative behavior, immediately deal with the behavior and calm the customer down before continuing the interaction. Maintain eye contact, be assertive, and speak in a controlled, authoritative tone. Offer a phrase of assurance: *"I'm going to take care of the problem for you right now."* If assuring doesn't calm the customer, address the combative behavior: *"I'm going to take care of this right away,* but I'll need you to speak more quietly so that I can understand you and find the best solution." If addressing the behavior directly doesn't stop the combativeness, get your supervisor involved. Don't try to handle a combative customer alone. It's not worth risking your own safety.

Identifying the Behavior

A combative customer may:

- Feel threatened.
- Resist any attempt to help.
- Be unable to control emotions.
- Unfairly blame others for problems.
- Be unwilling to take responsibility for behavior.
- Become belligerent.
- Argue, swear, accuse, or threaten you.
- Wring hands, flail arms, or gesture wildly.
- Get in your face.
- Get physically aggressive—if this happens, move away from the person and find someone in authority to help you.

Do This!

Robert is a flight attendant. He's been well trained to handle all types of passengers, including those who may be combative. During a cross-country flight, a passenger began acting out as soon as he boarded the plane. He tried getting up from his seat as they were taxiing but complied with Robert's announcement to sit down. The passenger then glared at him and became belligerent toward Robert as he walked through the cabin on his way to the galley.

Combative Passenger: "I need something to drink now!"

Employee: *"I understand, Sir.* As soon as we're at our flight altitude, we'll bring the food and beverage carts. Until then, *I'm sorry*, I'm not able to get you anything." **(empathy, courtesy, regret)**

Passenger: "I don't want it later. I need a drink now! I need to take my medication. This is ridiculous. Why can't you get me something now?!"

Employee: *"Sir,* it's against flight regulations. I'm not able to get anything from the galley now but as soon as I can, *I'll immediately bring you a glass of water so you can take your medicine."* (**courtesy, assurance**)

> (Robert paid close attention to the passenger's facial expressions and observed that the man was red faced and angry. Then he grabbed Robert's arm. Robert knew he needed to show the man that he was in charge and in control. So, rather than show alarm at the behavior, he maintained eye contact, calmly backed up a step, and moved his arm to release the man's grip.)

Passenger: "I don't want a glass of water. Bring me a scotch and soda!"

Employee: *"Yes Sir, I'll bring you your drink as soon as I can.* In the meantime I need you to stop getting physical with me. That's not acceptable."

Passenger: "Yeah, okay. Just bring me the drink when you can."

Why This Works

Robert never allowed the combative passenger to get the best of him. He maintained his composure, stayed calm, and spoke and acted in a controlled manner. When he first observed the combative behavior, he took immediate steps to stop it from escalating. When the man grabbed his arm, Robert did not act out. Rather, he calmly took a step back and removed his arm from the passenger's grasp. His confident demeanor followed by his authoritative words about the unacceptable behavior worked. Robert handled the situation effectively, but if his approach didn't calm the customer, he would have had to take other measures, such as getting the captain or a member of the flight crew to speak to the passenger. Robert was pleased that his confident, authoritative demeanor stopped the behavior, and that is always the number one goal when dealing with a combative person.

Applying the Approach

When handling a customer who is combative, apply the following principles to your situations:

- Pay close attention to a customer who appears angry, as anger is the most likely behavior to degrade into combativeness.

- Tune in to any customer who appears to be combative. Your immediate goal is to stop the behavior before he or she becomes verbally or physically aggressive.

- Maintain a positive attitude. Don't allow this type of customer to get to you or make you lose control of your emotions.

- Your actions are most important when dealing with a combative customer. Appearing confident and authoritative, maintaining eye contact, keeping a relaxed stance, and using an assertive tone of voice demonstrate that you are in control of the situation.

- At first, speak in a compassionate manner, using a phrase of empathy, such as *"I understand,"* as this may calm a customer, particularly if the behavior is fear driven.

- Let the customer know you're in control of the conversation through your tone of voice.

- Speak deliberately, respectfully, and authoritatively when you assure the customer that you are going to take care of the problem.

- Tell the customer what you're going to do to help.

- Don't get into an argument.

- If the customer doesn't calm down, state that you need him or her to stop the unacceptable behavior before you can continue the interaction.

- If that doesn't work, get your supervisor involved.

- If, at any time, you feel you're in danger, move quickly away from the customer and seek help.

What to Do When the Customer Is Condescending

A person who speaks in a condescending tone can be someone with a heightened sense of importance, someone who wants you to know exactly where you stand. People may also convey a condescending tone and demeanor when they lack confidence. These people put on airs to mask how they feel inside. No matter why someone speaks to you in a condescending tone, their behavior can push your buttons in a heartbeat. This type of customer is one of the most difficult to deal with because they act like they're better than you. They can easily get on your nerves to the point where you want to tell this type of person where to go! But, you know that as a frontline employee responsible for customer satisfaction it's your job to handle all your customers well, including those who speak condescendingly to you.

When you deal with a customer who is condescending, don't even attempt to change the person's behavior. Unlike someone who is angry or demanding or impatient, you aren't going to change this kind of behavior. Your best avenue is to stay on the high road, remind yourself that this person's behavior is no reflection on you, handle the customer to the best of your ability, keep your thoughts to yourself, and feel proud afterward that you didn't allow this customer to get to you and push your last button.

Identifying the Behavior

A condescending customer may:

- Display an air of superiority.
- Act in an arrogant manner.
- Be dismissive of others.

- Talk down to others.
- Be patronizing toward others.
- Order rather than ask.
- Act flippant.
- Belittle someone in earshot of others.
- Speak in an authoritative tone of voice.

Do This!

Brandon works as a concierge for an upscale hotel in Las Vegas. His job is to interact with the guests who have special requests and, in his two years on the job, he's handled all types of requests, not to mention all types of customers. One of the current guests, Mrs. Winfield, has tested his mettle, and he's trying his best not to let her get to him. He commented to his manager that this guest is the most difficult customer he's ever handled. She's only been a guest at the hotel for two days of a week-long stay, yet in that time he's complied to her requests for prime seats to shows that were sold out, gotten her the best tables in restaurants, had new pillows delivered when the ones on her bed weren't plump enough, and placated her when she complained that the maids were not respectful toward her. He just answered the phone and inwardly groaned when she introduced herself. It's only eight in the morning, and his first call of the day.

Condescending Customer: "Brandon, I know it's early but I've got a taste for sushi. I'd like you to have some delivered to my room—and none of those California rolls, or whatever you call them. I want only the best."

Employee: *"Good Morning, Mrs. Winfield. I'll be happy to have sushi delivered to your room; no California rolls. What types of sushi would you like?"* **(welcome, enthusiasm)**

Customer: "Now Brandon, as concierge, you should know what's best. Of course you probably haven't eaten sushi in Tokyo, where its absolutely the finest. Just get me the best you can find."

Employee: "*I'll take care of that right away, Mrs. Winfield, but it would help me if I knew more specifically what you like and how many people will be joining you. I don't want you to be disappointed.*" (**assurance, courtesy, rapport**)

Customer: "I like Ahi tuna . . . and perhaps some Bluefin. Nothing is going to compare with what we've been served on our frequent trips to Tokyo. I'll leave it up to you. And it's just for me, Brandon, so don't overdo it."

Employee: "*I can understand what you're saying about sushi in Tokyo. I'm proud to say that our sushi chef is from Tokyo. He's the expert so I'll explain what you like and leave the choices up to him. Does that sound all right?*" (**empathy, rapport**)

Customer: "Oh, he is? Well, he should know good sushi, then."

Employee: "*Great. I'll get this delivered to you right away. Thanks for giving me the opportunity to be of service this morning.*" (**enthusiasm, assurance, appreciation**)

Why This Works

You can imagine what Brandon was thinking when he took yet another call from the condescending Mrs. Winfield, who continually put on airs, talked down to him, and gave orders rather than asking for what she wanted. He knew that she considered him to be her personal assistant during her stay at the hotel and nothing in her attitude or demeanor was going to change. So, he ignored her air of superiority and condescending comments, handled her request with confidence, stayed in control of the conversation, and worked through the steps of the interaction efficiently and effectively. By interjecting powerful phrases throughout the conversation, and maintaining a great attitude, he conducted himself in a professional, dignified manner, and he didn't allow her to get on his last nerve.

Quick Tip for a Sticky Situation

You may be able to put yourself on a level playing field with someone who's condescending by presenting yourself as confident, self-assured, and nonplussed by the person's behavior. Even if the person doesn't warm up to you, continue to handle yourself in the same, professional manner you would use with anyone else. Then pat yourself on the back for staying on the high road.

Applying the Approach

When handling a customer who is condescending toward you, apply the following principles to your situations:

- You'll most likely witness the condescension from the moment you begin handling this type customer. Consider that acting this way is how they treat everyone in a service position.

- Intersperse phrases of welcome, courtesy, enthusiasm, assurance, empathy, regret, and appreciation throughout your conversation as you work through the six steps to successfully handle the customer.

- Asking *How are you doing today?* may not help establish a rapport, but at least you tried. The best way to establish a rapport with this type of personality is to stay professional and present a great attitude.

- Never speak in a condescending tone to someone who is condescending; speak in your normal tone of voice.

- Ignore the condescending behavior; act as you do with any customer.

- Don't allow a condescending person to make you feel belittled or demeaned.

- The more confident and self-assured you are, the less you'll be bothered by condescending people.

What to Do When the Customer
Is Confused

Customers may be confused for a number of reasons. The most obvious reason is that the customer simply does not understand what you're saying. A language or accent barrier may cause a disconnect in communication. Perhaps you're speaking in technical or company terms that don't mean anything to the customer. Perhaps the customer has zero understanding of the product or service you're talking about. Or, perhaps, the customer has a medical condition that makes communication and understanding difficult.

Something about the customer's facial expression will usually be your first signal of confusion. When a customer looks at you with the bewildered, perplexed, or blank look that tells you he or she has no clue what you're saying, back up for a moment and try to figure out the cause for the confusion. If a language barrier exists, speak slowly and use easy-to-understand words. Showing or pointing to the details on the item as you're talking can help clear up confusion as well, since the customer is receiving both audio and visual signals. If you speak with an accent and the customer is having a difficult time understanding you, look directly at him or her, slow your speech, and enunciate clearly. If you're talking over the customer's head, and he or she doesn't have a clue what you're saying, repeating verbatim isn't going to clear up the confusion. You'll need to phrase what you've already said in a different way. If you've identified that the customer is confused because of a medical condition, again speak slowly and clearly, use easy-to-understand words and phrases, and ask questions to make sure the customer is staying with you throughout the conversation.

Identifying the Behavior

A confused customer may:

- Look bewildered or perplexed.
- Seem disoriented or mixed up.
- Not make eye contact.
- Nod frequently.
- Readily agree with what you're saying.
- Be embarrassed and not ask questions for the fear of sounding dumb.
- Phrase statements as questions.
- Ask questions that don't pertain to the conversation.
- Be unable to answer questions.
- Give vague or one word answers to questions.
- Speak in a manner that signals a medical condition that makes communication difficult .

Do This!

Kevin owns a guitar store. He's been playing guitar since he was a young child, has a degree in music, and is considered an expert in his community. In addition to managing the store, Kevin plays in a band and gives guitar lessons. He loves talking guitar and helping fellow musicians. Most of his customers have played before, are knowledgeable about guitars, and have a good idea of what they want. Until today.

Employee: *"Good Afternoon. Welcome to Baker Guitars. How can I help you today?"* **(welcome)**

Confused Customer: "Hi. I'm interested in buying a guitar. I came here because my friend said you're the expert."

Employee: *"Oh, thanks, but I don't know about that. My name is Kevin, and I'll be happy to help you. How are you doing?"* **(courtesy, rapport, welcome, enthusiasm, rapport)**

Customer: "I'm OK. How are you?"

Employee: "I'm doing well, *thanks*. Are you looking for an acoustic or an electric guitar?" **(courtesy)**

Customer: "Umm . . . electric."

Employee: *"Great! I can help you with that. Mind if I ask your name?"* **(enthusiasm, courtesy)**

Customer: "Susan."

Employee: *"Thanks, Susan. Let me show you what we have in the way of electric guitars. What's your price range?"* **(courtesy)**

Customer: "I hadn't thought about that."

Employee: "The prices range from less than a hundred for this one, to over a thousand for this one."

Customer: "This one is pretty."

Employee: *"It sure is. Let me get it down so you can see how it feels."* **(rapport)**

> (As Kevin helped Susan slip the guitar over her head, he got the feeling that she didn't know a lot about guitars and, reflecting on her comment that he was the expert, he wondered if she may have even felt a little intimidated.)

Employee: "How does that feel?"

Customer: "Good."

Employee: "The body looks like it'll be comfortable for you. What about the fret placement? Try strumming and see how it feels."

> (Susan had a bewildered look on her face as she looked at the guitar, and Kevin's suspicions were confirmed. She seemed confused when he mentioned the frets. Not wanting to embarrass her, Kevin switched gears, went back to Step 3 to make sure he understood what she really wanted and needed in a guitar.)

Employee: "Let's hang this one back up. I'd like to ask you a couple questions before we go further. What type of music do you like to play?"

Customer: "Umm, I like all kinds."

Employee: *"Well, I like to listen to all kinds of music. But when it comes to guitar playing, I play rock, so an electric guitar suits me best. For people who prefer playing, say, pop or country, an acoustic guitar often is best. And for someone just starting out, I always suggest they start with a low-priced acoustic, because an acoustic is a great way to learn guitar."* **(rapport)**

Customer: "I guess you figured out I haven't played a guitar before. I just didn't want to look dumb."

Employee: *"You didn't, but I've been there, and I certainly under-stand that feeling. I didn't always know a lot about guitars either. I have a couple more questions and then I'll get you set up with the guitar that'll best suit you."* **(empathy, rapport, assurance)**

Why This Works

Kevin could have sold Susan the electric guitar she thought was pretty, put the money in the bank, and not thought any more of the interaction. But would Susan have been satisfied? Probably not, especially once she realized that what she thought she wanted, based on the prettiness factor, wasn't the best style for her needs. This interaction worked because Kevin paid attention, listened well, quickly sized up the situation, and realized that Susan was confused. Most important, this worked because he did not embarrass her or make her feel stupid, but rather worked on building a rapport to increase her comfort level. He took a step back in handling her request and asked her more questions to ensure he had a good understanding of what would be best for her.

The most important goal, when handling a customer who's confused, is to determine the cause of the confusion—in Susan's case, it was being unfamiliar with the product—and clearing up the confusion before proceeding in the steps of handling the customer. Think of it this way: a confused customer is likely to be embarrassed, may try to act like he or she knows what you're talking about, and agree with your proposed solution, but ultimately won't be satisfied if your proposed solution isn't on target.

Applying the Approach

When handling a customer who is confused, apply the following principles to your situations:

- When someone is confused, he or she is also likely to feel embarrassed and will try to mask the confusion.

- You probably won't recognize the confusion immediately, unless a language or accent barrier exists, which will make normal communication nearly impossible.

- If you suspect the customer is confused, pay close attention to body language and facial expressions.

- In the event that the customer is confused because of a lack of knowledge or experience about the product or service, you're likely to discover the confusion when you're in Step 3, Understanding the Customer's Request, or Step 4, Assisting the Customer.

- Something that the customer says or doesn't say is going to signal confusion. When you notice that, ask more questions to make sure that you understand the request and that the customer understands your questions.

- Establishing a rapport is a great way to get a confused customer on your side. By lessening the feelings of embarrassment, the customer will begin to open up and you'll get the answers to your questions that will help you understand the request.

- When a language or accent barrier exists, speak slowly and clearly, using easy-to-understand words.

- If you discover that you've been speaking company-ese, or using technical or slang words, rephrase what you've already said using plain English and good grammar.

- If you've said something a couple times and the customer still appears confused, say it again using different phrases that may be more easily understood.

- If a medical condition makes communicating difficult, it may be helpful to use visual aids, such as drawing, or by writing down the key points for the customer.

- Always make sure you clear up the confusion before completing the interaction so that you are confident in finding the best solution.

- Never belittle a customer for being confused. Doing so will only add to the customer's embarrassment, and you're apt to lose this customer.

What to Do When the Customer Is a Deal Maker

Some customers love the challenge of making a deal. Deal makers are smooth talkers who don't like to take no for an answer. They want to come out on top and they like to win. They may turn on the charm to try to get you to agree with them, or they may try to guilt you into agreeing with them.

Unless you work in a field where dealing is considered normal, such as a car dealership, handling someone who wants to negotiate and try to get you to deviate from usual business procedures isn't all that difficult. You just need to be politely firm. If your company has set prices and policies for all customers, the best way to handle a deal maker is to courteously and assertively stand your ethical ground. Phrases of empathy may be useful, such as, *"I can relate. I'd like that deal myself, and I wish I could do it for you."* Then follow up with a phrase of assurance: *"Here's what I can do."* Stating this phrase assertively in a positive, enthusiastic tone of voice puts you back in the driver's seat and in control of the conversation.

Identifying the Behavior

A deal maker customer may:

- Love the challenge of wheeling and dealing.
- Want to come out on top.
- Not like to lose.
- Consider himself or herself to be a good negotiator.
- Love to haggle.
- Like to circumvent the rules.
- Feel that rules are for everyone else.

- Be shrewd or unscrupulous.
- Be smooth talking.
- Turn on the charm when wheeling and dealing.
- Become jazzed up or excited when trying to strike a deal.
- Try to get you to agree through mild coercion.
- Try to make you feel sorry or guilty if you don't agree.

Do This!

James is an estimator for a national moving company. Most customers accept his proposals but today the customer he's handling wants to negotiate the rate.

Deal Maker Customer: "Geez, James, that sounds like an awful lot of moolah just to move my measly belongings. Can't you do a little better?"

Employee: *"I know that moving is tough enough, let alone all the costs involved with it.* Based on your belongings, packing the boxes, and the distance you're moving, this is the estimated cost. Here's the pledge our company offers. If, when the truck is weighed, it's heavier than what I estimated based on the items that are listed, you won't be charged any extra." **(empathy)**

Customer: "Oh, okay. My stuff probably doesn't weigh that much. How about shaving some of those pounds you estimated? I'll buy you lunch if you can do that."

Employee: *"I'm not able to do that. We pride ourselves on giving fair estimates to each of our customers. Here's what I can do for you. If you'd like to pack your own belongings rather than pay us to do it, I'll be happy to rework the estimate."* **(empathy, assurance, enthusiasm)**

Customer: "I have a bad knee so I can't do that. Isn't there a special rate for people like me who have a problem?"

Employee: *"I feel for you, Mr. Davis. I'd like to say yes, but the esti-mate I gave you is the best I can do. What we offer to one cus-*

tomer is what we offer to all customers. As I said, if I underestimated the weight, you won't be charged anything additional for my error. I'm just not able to make an error like that on purpose. *I'm sure you understand why."* **(empathy, courtesy, assurance, rapport)**

Customer: "Well, you can't blame a guy for trying. Where do I sign?"

Why This Works

When he realized Mr. Davis was a wheeler dealer, James didn't back down. He was firm, yet courteous in his responses. Mr. Davis tried to wear him down with an offer to buy lunch, and then tried to play on his sympathies about the bad knee, but James stood his ground. He didn't belabor the methods Mr. Davis was employing, such as getting into discussions about the proposed bribe or supposed bad knee, but rather moved through the interaction by using phrases of empathy and assurance. James focused on what he could do rather than on what he couldn't do, which kept him in control of the conversation. He also related the ethical standards of his company and demonstrated, through his words and actions, that he was an ethical employee.

Applying the Approach

When handling a customer who is a deal maker, apply the following principles to your situations:

- You may encounter deal making behavior when you're in Step 4, Assist the Customer. After proposing your best solution, this type customer is going to want a better deal, a special favor, or something additional for nothing.
- After you've made your proposal, the deal making begins.
- This might be a game for this type person who loves the bargain-

ing part of making any deal. When you recognize this behavior, take firm steps to nip it in the bud, otherwise you'll never get to Step 5, Gain Agreement.

- Don't let a customer cajole you into agreeing to a special deal that you don't offer all customers.

- Don't let a customer make you feel guilty by sharing something personal in the hopes of playing on your sympathy and getting you to back down.

- Offering a phrase of empathy, such as, *"I'm with you on that. I'd like to be able to make that deal, but . . . ,"* will often let the customer know you understand.

- Then, adding a phrase of assurance, *"here's what I can do for you,"* gives you back the control to affirm your best solution and gain agreement.

- Keep a friendly facial expression, smile as appropriate, make eye contact when you speak, and maintain a relaxed demeanor. In other words, don't show a deal maker that you are flustered or put off by the behavior.

- Conducting yourself in an ethical manner sends a clear message to a wheeler dealer type of person that you aren't a pushover.

- Conducting yourself in an ethical manner also sends a positive message to you because you can feel proud that you stayed on track and did the right thing.

What to Do When the Customer Is Demanding

You'll recognize demanding customers by the way in which they present their request or problem to you. They'll likely tell rather than ask. They'll expect you to give them more than is required. They'll ask for and expect special favors and may even expect you to jump through hoops just for them. They don't care that you have other customers or that your company prides itself on acting ethically by treating all customers fairly and equitably. You'll recognize demanding customers because they're the ones who make you want to ask, "Just who do you think you are?"

Demanding customers don't care about other customers, or you, for that matter. They have unrealistic or unreasonable service expectations and still want more. They want what they want, and that usually means now. Turning around this type of behavior is possible, but you'll need to put on your kid gloves. It's important that you treat a demanding customer with respect, using powerful phrases of courtesy, enthusiasm, assurance, and empathy. You want to get your point across that you treat all your customers the same, yet you also want to make this customer feel valued. Difficult? Yes. Possible? Definitely yes!

Identifying the Behavior

A demanding customer may:

- Have unreasonable expectations.
- Expect more than is due them.
- Expect 110 percent from everyone.
- Are often good manipulators.

- Tell rather than ask.
- Be difficult to satisfy.
- Be assertive or aggressive in their approach.
- Not take the time for pleasantries or courtesies.
- Be forceful when stating needs.
- Ask for special favors.
- Want freebies and discounts.
- Expect you to jump through hoops.
- May threaten to take business elsewhere if demands aren't met.
- Not care about other customers.
- Be self-serving or selfish by nature.
- Expect a lot done in a short time.
- Like to win.

Do This!

Debbie works as a pharmacy tech for a drug store chain. She's responsible for checking in phone and walk-in customers, entering the prescription information into the computer, and checking customers out. When she saw Mr. Stiles walk toward the check-in counter, she groaned, remembering that last month he talked her into doing a special favor by filling his prescription ahead of other waiting customers. She suspects he's going to have the same expectation today.

Employee: *"Good Morning, Mr. Stiles. How are you doing?"* **(welcome)**

Demanding Customer: "Hi Debbie, I'm doing good, thanks. Hey, I'm in a hurry, and I need this prescription filled fast."

Employee: *"I'll be happy to get it filled for you.* Right now we're pretty backed up, so the soonest we can get it done is around four this afternoon." **(enthusiasm)**

Customer: "Oh no, that won't work. I need it right now."

Employee: *"I understand, and I'd like to do it for you right now.* We have to fill the prescriptions in order, though, *and realistically the soonest I can guarantee is around four this afternoon.* **(empathy, rapport, assurance)**

Customer: "You did it for me last month, and I'm sure other people were waiting then. Look I get all my prescriptions filled here, and I like you guys. There are other pharmacies, and if I don't get good service here I may have to go somewhere else."

Employee: *"Mr. Stiles, I remember what I did for you last month, and I'd love to be able to help you out again, but that wouldn't be fair to our other customers who are already waiting. If I were to fill someone else's order ahead of yours, that wouldn't be fair to you either. I'll tell you what, if we can get it filled earlier, I'll be happy to call you. Look, I really do understand where you're coming from and I hope you understand my position too."* **(courtesy, rapport, assurance, enthusiasm, empathy, rapport)**

Customer: "Well, if there's nothing you can do . . . try to get it earlier for me if you can, okay?"

Employee: *"I sure will.* I'll call you if it's done early. *Thanks for understanding and thanks for your business. We do appreciate you."* **(enthusiasm, appreciation)**

Why This Works

This worked because Debbie didn't back down. She wished she hadn't set the precedent for a special favor the prior month, so she had to figure out a way to stop the demanding behavior. She interspersed phrases of courtesy, rapport, enthusiasm, assurance, and empathy throughout her conversation as she explained why the special favor could not be repeated. When Mr. Stiles commented he would take his business elsewhere, Debbie ignored that statement, rather addressing it during her phrase of appreciation, when she thanked the customer for his business and told him she appreciated him. Debbie worked on building a rapport by relating the situation if it were reversed, and that helped him see the situation from a different perspective. She even went a step further and offered to call him if the prescription was filled early, which made him feel valued.

Quick Tip for a Sticky Situation

Customers who do a lot of business with your company may develop a sense of entitlement and become demanding. They want special treatment in exchange for their loyalty. And for high-volume customers, it might make good business sense to appease them and meet their demands. But this shouldn't be your call. As a frontline employee you need to focus on ethical treatment and doing what's right for all your customers. Your manager or owner needs to make the call for repeat customers who become demanding.

Applying the Approach

When handling a customer who is demanding, apply the following principles to your situations:

- A demanding customer is still your customer and should be treated with respect and courtesy.
- Your responsibility is to handle every customer ethically, and that means fairly.
- Pay attention and listen to the customer's demand. This will give you time to formulate your response.
- Choose positive words and phrases of enthusiasm by focusing on what you "can" do for this customer.
- It may help to frame the demand from a different perspective, as Debbie did when she explained that he wouldn't like it if she handled another customer ahead of him.

- Smile and maintain a friendly, positive attitude.

- Don't get into an arguing match with a demanding customer. State your ethical position and stand your ground.

- If a demanding customer threatens to go elsewhere, it's best to ignore the statement. If you say something like, "Go ahead," you're not giving the customer the opportunity to save face, and you might lose this customer. Rather, address it during your phrase of appreciation and tell the customer that you do indeed appreciate his or her business.

- If a demanding customer doesn't back down and asks for a manager, by all means, get your manager to make the call.

What to Do When the Customer Is Demeaning (to You Personally)

It's never all right to demean or belittle someone, but you know it happens. Some people feel the need to put others down. It's happened to all of us at some point in our lives. Someone said something that was so demeaning it made you feel terrible. Perhaps it was a comment about your weight, your hair, your clothes, your teeth, your health, or your actions. The words flew out of the person's mouth with the ease of a kite floating on a spring day, but they hit you with the power of an arrow shooting straight to your core. You may have felt indignant, defensive, and wanted to tell the person off, or you may felt humiliated and allowed the words to damage your self-esteem.

When a customer demeans you, it's how you react that can make the difference between handling this type of customer professionally or feeling so flustered that you allow the demeaning words to dictate your handling of the interaction. First and most important: Never allow anyone's demeaning words to damage your self-esteem. The best way to reply to a demeaning comment may be to say nothing and let the words roll off your back like water on a duck. If you feel a comment is warranted, just say something like, "*Thank you* for telling me," or "*Thank you* for the advice." Then decide for yourself whether or not you want to accept the advice or let it go in one ear and out the other. Of course that's a lot easier said than done. But you have to remind yourself that people who demean others don't really have other people's best interests in mind. If they did, they'd find a kinder, gentler way to offer helpful advice—or better yet, they'd keep their unsolicited advice to themselves. Bottom line is that when a person demeans another, that person has a skewed sense of self; in other words, it's really all about the person saying the words, not the recipient.

Identifying the Behavior

A demeaning customer may:

- Have a sense of self-importance and feel the right to criticize or belittle others.
- Have a misguided sense about how to be helpful.
- Feel the need to offer unsolicited advice.
- Not realize how hurtful the words are.
- Be a controlling type of person.
- Be judgmental or intolerant of others who are different.
- Not be nice to anyone.
- Be unhappy and want to bring others down.
- Be insecure and point out others' shortcomings to make themselves feel better.

Do This!

Julie works as a barista in a coffee shop and handles the early morning crowd on their way to the commuter train station. She's been overweight since she was a young child. She's tried dieting, joined weight loss clubs, and signed up for weight loss programs. She's also joined gyms and even hired a personal trainer, but she's never been able to stick to any program and her weight issues have become an ongoing battle. Consequently, Julie is insecure about her weight and her self-esteem, but she tries to overcome her insecurities through her friendly, outgoing personality.

Employee: *Good Morning, how are you doing today?"* **(welcome, rapport)**

Demeaning Customer: "Great, thanks."

Employee: *"What can I get for you?"* **(welcome)**

Customer: "I'll have a large nonfat cinnamon dulce latte, no whipped cream."

Employee: *"Excellent! That sounds good!* Would you like anything with that?" **(enthusiasm, rapport)**

Customer: "No, I don't need the extra calories. I try to watch what I eat. You know, it doesn't look like you do, though. You'd be really pretty if you lost some weight."

> (Julie ignored the comment, smiled at the customer, and went on with her conversation.)

Employee: "That'll be $4.65, *please."* **(courtesy)**

Customer: "Here you go. I mean it. If you lost weight you'd be very pretty."

Employee: "Here's your change, and *thank you* for the advice. Your latte will be up in a minute, and *thank you for coming in today."* **(courtesy, appreciation)**

Why This Works

When Julie didn't respond to the customer's comment, he persisted. She knew she'd need to address it, so she thanked him for giving her advice rather than putting him down or defending herself, which would have prolonged the conversation about her weight. Julie could have stooped to his level by commenting, "And what about that beer gut you're toting around?" The customer would likely have become offended and may have said something even more demeaning to her. Or she could have belittled herself by saying, "I know I'm overweight. I'm keep trying to lose, but I have such a hard time. It's really tough, especially working here with all the yummy coffee drinks I just can't avoid." The customer would likely have continued to give her unsolicited advice, making her feel even worse. When Julie said *"Thank you* for your advice," there was nothing more for him to say.

Applying the Approach

When handling a customer who is demeaning, apply the following principles to your situations:

- Even though you may want to and feel it's warranted, don't demean a customer who demeans you.

- Consider that this customer is someone who likes to feel he or she is in control, is better than others, is judgmental, and has the need to 'help' others by giving unsolicited advice.

- This is really hard to do, but try not to take any demeaning comment personally. Consider that this person is likely to be this way to everyone; in other words, he or she is not a kind, considerate person.

- When someone demeans your physical appearance, such as in the example above, at the most, say, "*thank you* for your advice," or "*thank you* for letting me know." Don't feel you have to explain yourself. You don't.

- When someone demeans your outward appearance, such as, "What did you do, take a bath in that perfume?" Say something like, "*I'm sorry that it's offensive to you.*" Then decide whether or not to accept the feedback. If you can't decide whether it's valid, ask a trusted friend.

- When someone demeans your health by saying something like, "You should quit smoking. It makes your breath stink. Not to mention, it's really bad for you," let's face it: if you're a smoker, you already know that it's bad for your health. If a person chooses to demean you about it, you could make direct eye contact and acknowledge the statement: "You're not telling me anything I don't already know or think about every day. But *thank you* for reminding me." Then move on to helping the customer.

- When someone is angry about something you or your company did and says something that demeans your actions, such as, "You must be really stupid for doing that!", consider that this person is demeaning you as the representative of your company, not you personally. Don't even address the comment. Continue with your conversation, speaking in a calm voice, following the tips to help a customer who is angry.

- No matter the reason why someone demeans you, don't allow that one comment get to you. Speak in a respectful tone of voice and maintain an open, relaxed demeanor. Act confidently.

- Smile and mentally remind yourself of your value and worth. Take the high road and maintain a positive attitude.

- Make eye contact when you speak to demeaning people, especially if you are thanking them for the (unsolicited) advice. And when you thank them, use a neutral tone of voice.

- Never agree or put yourself down to a customer who has demeaned you.

- Always treat everyone with dignity and respect, even when people don't treat you this way.

What to Do When the Customer Is Dismissive

Like condescending customers, those who are dismissive toward you can quickly push your buttons. They may talk on their cell phone while you're trying to help, have a simultaneous conversation with another person, or ignore you completely. You get the feeling they think that what they're doing is more important than what you're doing. And you're trying to help them! They come across as arrogant, disrespectful, or feeling superior to others, when they may actually just be overworked or stressed and trying to multitask at an inappropriate time. It's best not to judge someone who's dismissive, because the person may not realize he or she is behaving this way.

The best way to handle someone who treats you in a dismissive manner is to ignore the behavior and go about your business of handling the customer's request, interrupting courteously and assertively when you need to ask a question or when you're presenting your solution. It's going to be tough to try to build a rapport with a customer who's acting dismissively toward you. If this behavior continues, you may decide to excuse yourself until the customer is ready to pay attention, using a phrase of courtesy and a phrase of enthusiasm: *"Excuse me, I'll be happy to help you as soon as you're ready"* and moving on to another task, paying attention, and making yourself available when the customer is ready to be helped.

Identifying the Behavior

A dismissive customer may:

- Come across as arrogant.
- Be disrespectful toward others.

- Feel superior toward others.
- Have a disregard for service personnel.
- Feel that what he or she is doing is more important.
- Be aloof or standoffish.
- Be preoccupied by or worried about something.
- Be multitasking and not realize he or she is acting dismissively.
- Not care that you or other customers are waiting.
- Hold a conversation with another person while you're trying to help.
- Not make eye contact.
- Use hand gestures or facial expressions to convey a message.
- Ignore you completely.

Do This!

Craig is employed by the U.S. Postal Service as a customer service employee. He enjoys working the counter and while he enjoys talking to customers, those who talk on their cell phones really tick him off, especially since his supervisor posted a sign for customers to finish their cell phone calls before approaching the counter. He feels these types of customers have little regard for him and treat him disrespectfully. He spoke to his supervisor, who gave him some tips for handling these types of customers. He's about to see if the supervisor's tips work.

Employee: *"Good morning, how can I help you?"* **(welcome)**

> (Craig smiled and ignored the fact that the customer walked up to the counter with a cell phone attached to his ear.)

Dismissive Customer: "John, hold on a second. No, no. Hold on just a sec. I'm at the post office. Hi, I need to get this package mailed. John, I'm back. Go ahead. . . ."

Employee: *"Excuse me, Sir,* how do you want this mailed? Priority or parcel post?" **(courtesy)**

Customer: "I'm sorry, John. Need you to hold on again. Uh, priority. Okay, I'm back. . . ."

Employee: *"Thanks, I'll be happy to take care of that for you.* Anything liquid, perishable, fragile, or potentially hazardous?" **(courtesy, enthusiasm)**

> (When Craig asked this question the customer merely shook his head, continuing his cell phone conversation.)

Employee: "And do you need insurance or delivery confirmation?"

> (The customer mouthed that he wanted delivery confirmation.)

Employee: *"Thank you.* The total will be "25.85, *please.*"**(courtesy)**

Customer: "John, hold on again. I need to put the cell phone down a sec while I get my wallet out. I'll be right back. How much was it?"

Employee: "25.85, *please.*" **(courtesy)**

Customer: "Here's $30."

Employee: *"Thank you.* Here's your change and *thanks for your business."* **(courtesy, appreciation)**

Why This Works

When Craig talked to his supervisor about these types of situations, his supervisor suggested that the best way to handle customers who were dismissive was to smile, speak courteously, and ignore the behavior. Craig felt good after handling this customer because he kept his cool, didn't say anything rude to the customer, and did his best to handle the request efficiently and correctly. He didn't try to build a rapport because he knew that wouldn't be possible, but relied instead on phrases of courtesy and enthusiasm while he took care of the request. Because he was able to quickly complete the request, Craig handled this customer well.

Quick Tip for a Sticky Situation

If a customer you're attempting to help is speaking on a cell phone and, like Craig, you can complete the transaction by communicating through facial expressions and hand signals, that's great. But if you need more than hand signals to communicate and other customers are waiting in line, politely say to the dismissive customer, "*Ms. Customer,* other customers are waiting to be helped. Rather than make them wait while you finish your phone call, *I'll be happy to take care of your request as soon as you're done.*" Give her the opportunity to end the call, and if she doesn't, smile and courteously say to the next person in line, "*May I help you?*" Then when the dismissive customer finishes the call resume your contact. This may change her demeanor from dismissive to agitated or angry, so nip that behavior in the bud by saying, "*Thank you so much for understanding that other people were waiting to be helped. I appreciate that you allowed me to help one of them while you finished your call.*"

Applying the Approach

When handling a customer who is dismissive, apply the following principles to your situations:

- If you don't need the customer's input to complete the request, ignore the behavior and continue working.
- Deal with this type of customer by being pleasant and polite.
- Use phrases of courtesy throughout your conversation whenever you need the customer's attention.

- Maintain a good attitude. Don't allow someone who's dismissive toward you to change your attitude.

- Smile, choose positive words.

- Maintain a friendly facial expression, look at the customer when you speak, and act assertively when you need to ask a question or offer your solution.

- Speak in a helpful tone of voice.

- Assume that the customer may not realize he or she is behaving dismissively so don't take the behavior personally.

- Handle the request as you would any customer, unless other customers are waiting, as previously explained.

- If you excuse yourself to handle another customer, use a phrase of courtesy and a phrase of enthusiasm when you return to the dismissive customer: *"Thanks so much for understanding that another customer was waiting. I'll be happy to help you now."*

What to Do When the Customer Is Dissatisfied (with You or Your Company)

Unlike an angry customer whom you can calm down and get on your side to complete the interaction successfully, a customer dissatisfied with your proposed solutions or who refuses your help altogether can be particularly tough to handle. Perhaps at some point during your interaction you sensed the customer was going to be difficult to please. Perhaps you thought you were successfully handling the customer, but the customer isn't agreeing to any of your proposed solutions. Perhaps the customer is so upset by an error caused by your company that he or she immediately asks for a supervisor. And, some customers just can't be pleased no matter how hard you try.

Satisfying a customer who can't be satisfied isn't impossible. Presenting yourself as confident and competent is the key to handling these types of people. Phrases of assurance, such as, *"I'm going to find a way to resolve this to your satisfaction,"* or *"Please give me the opportunity to fix this for you,"* are crucial. Attentiveness actions are also important. Focus solely on the customer, make eye contact, listen actively to what the customer says, and carefully observe his or her facial expressions and body language. Phrases of assurance and attentive actions will often put you on different footing with a customer who's dissatisfied because you demonstrate, through your words and actions, that you're capable, competent, and want to help. The way you present yourself can often change the customer's behavior, and they may begin trusting you to find the best solution.

Identifying the Behavior

A dissatisfied customer may:

- Have unrealistic expectations.
- Be displeased with all your suggestions.
- Keep saying no.
- Display body language such as arms crossed in front of the body and stiff demeanor.
- Not listen to what you're offering.
- Talk over you when you're trying to offer a solution.
- Immediately ask to speak to a supervisor.
- Demand to speak to the CEO.
- Threaten to take business elsewhere.

Do This!

Matthew has worked for a major telecommunications company for nine years, handling customer service in the repair department. He understands that working for a utility is tough because people have preconceived ideas that service will be poor. Matthew prides himself on having developed the skills to handle any type customer in any situation, including those who aren't easily satisfied. As he answers each phone call with the company's standard greeting, he wonders what type of problem and what type of customer he's going to encounter.

Employee: *"Good morning, my name is Matthew. May I have your telephone number please and name please?"* **(welcome, courtesy)**

Dissatisfied Customer: "It's 555-5382. My name is Mr. Irwin. Let me speak to a supervisor."

Employee: *"I'll be happy to get a supervisor to help you, but will* *you please tell me the reason you're calling?"* **(enthusiasm, assurance, courtesy)**

Customer: "Yes. You guys just can't get my phone line fixed. I keep reporting static on my line. You've been out three times, and it's back again."

Employee: *"I'm terribly sorry that's happening. Mr. Irwin, I can get my supervisor to help you, but first I'd like to see what's going on. I'm sure I'll be able to take care of this to your satisfaction."* **(regret, courtesy, assurance)**

Customer: "I've called and talked to you guys too many times already. I really want to speak to a supervisor."

Employee: *"I understand where you're coming from. But I haven't been involved with your situation. I'm confident I'll be able to help you, but if I can't find a workable solution, I'll explain the situation to my supervisor and let her handle this for you."* **(empathy, assurance)**

Customer: "Okay. I'll give you one more shot. But don't dog this or just tell me something you think I want to hear. I'm at the point where I'm ready to call the public service commission to report your company's incompetence."

Employee: *"I understand. Believe me, I wouldn't be happy either. But I appreciate you giving me the opportunity to take care of this for you.* What I'd like to do, *with your permission*, is research what's happened so far and speak to the field supervisor to find out what we're going to do to fix this problem permanently. Then, *I can give you a realistic time frame.* If that's acceptable to you, *Mr. Irwin, I'll call you back within one hour and let you know how we're going to resolve this."* **(empathy, rapport, appreciation, courtesy, assurance, courtesy, assurance)**

Customer: "All right. But just to let you know, if I don't hear from you in an hour I'm calling the public service commission."

Employee: *"Yes, Sir. I will definitely call you back within one hour."* **(courtesy, enthusiasm, assurance)**

(After speaking with the field supervisor, Matthew called Mr. Irwin back.)

Employee: *"Mr. Irwin, this is Matthew. I just spoke to the field supervisor and explained what's been going on with your phone line.* He looked into the problem and since we haven't been able to get rid of the static by trying to fix the line going into your home, *he's going to have a crew out tomorrow morning to lay a new cable into your home. He's regrets that his crew hasn't fixed the problem, and he's confident this will take care of it for good. We do appreciate you as our customer, and I also want to assure you that I'm going to speak to my supervisor and let her know what's happened. My personal extension is 3342. Please contact me directly if you need to call back for any reason."* **(courtesy, welcome, assurance, enthusiasm, regret, appreciation, assurance)**

Why This Works

Unlike an angry customer you can calm down by offering a phrase of regret followed by a phrase of assurance, a dissatisfied customer most likely has already been an angry customer, has already been apologized to and has received assurances that the problem will be handled. That customer is now at the point of wanting a supervisor, severing the business relationship, or reporting the complaint to a higher authority. Matthew understands his customers and didn't get flustered or upset by Mr. Irwin, who was so dissatisfied Matthew knew it would be a huge hurdle just to get him on his side.

Matthew was calm and demonstrated through phrases of assurance spoken in a confident tone that he was capable and interested in resolving the problem. He came across as concerned and showed he understood this was an urgent situation requiring immediate handling. He ignored Mr. Irwin's threats and, instead, worked to resolve the problem. When he called Mr. Irwin back and explained what they were going to do, Mr. Irwin felt comfortable with the resolution. Then Matthew went a couple steps further by stating that he was going to make his supervisor aware of the problem and he gave Mr. Irwin his personal extension, which conveyed a positive message to the customer.

Quick Tip for a Sticky Situation

If you've exhausted all solutions and can't find any that the customer will agree to, ask him or her to help you find a workable solution that is fair to both your company and to him or her. By stressing "fair to both company and customer," you let the customer know that asking for the moon isn't going to be a plausible end result. Together, try to come to terms for a workable solution. Then, if you still can't satisfy this person, get your supervisor involved.

Applying the Approach

When handling a customer who is dissatisfied, apply the following principles to your situations:

- Put all your verbal skills to good use: phrases of courtesy, enthusiasm, assurance, empathy, regret, and appreciation. In other words, convey your ability to confidently and competently handle the problem to satisfactory resolution.
- Put all nonverbal skills to good use: pay complete attention, listen closely, believe that you can make a difference, choose positive words, focus on what you can do, keep an open mind, assume the customer has good reason for the dissatisfaction, maintain a concerned facial expression and tone of voice and, most important, project confidence.
- Assure the customer that the buck stops with you.
- Empathize, as that often gets a customer on your side.

- Make very sure you understand completely the reason the customer is dissatisfied before attempting to help.
- Then quickly work to find a solution that will satisfy this customer.
- Throughout the interaction, remain calm and in control.
- Display confidence and competence.
- If at any time, you determine that the customer doesn't feel comfortable allowing you to handle the problem, get your supervisor to handle the customer.

What to Do When the Customer Is Freaking Out

A person loses control when fear becomes irrational or uncontrolled. He or she is unable to stay composed, can no longer think logically or function rationally, and becomes unglued, hysterical, or paranoid. Sometimes people lose control to the point of freaking out before a medical or dental procedure. People who suffer from panic attacks may lose control when in an unfamiliar or uncomfortable environment. People who are mentally unstable may be prone to losing control without warning (this type of behavior will be covered separately on pages **000-000**).

Let's hope you never encounter a customer whose behavior has deteriorated to the point he or she loses control and freaks out. But you may, particularly if you work in the medical or dental field. Your number one goal is to get the individual to calm down or you won't be able to proceed. Phrases of empathy and assurance are your allies when dealing with someone who's losing it. Empathize and speak in a kind manner: *"I've been in your shoes, and I know how you feel."* Encourage the person to breathe slowly and deeply. Assure by calmly explaining what you're going to do: *"Let me explain the steps of the procedure. . . ."* Gain agreement, then proceed slowly, gauging the person's calmness level and taking short breaks if you feel that will help. If you can't help the customer or patient calm down, ask for your manager's (or the doctor's or dentist's) help. Never continue with the interaction until the person assures you he or she is calm enough for you to proceed.

Identifying the Behavior

A customer or patient who is freaking out may:

- Be extremely frightened.
- Be unable to control emotions.
- Not think logically.
- Display irrational behavior.
- Act paranoid.
- Become hysterical.
- Scream or yell.
- Lose it completely.
- Become physical.

Do This!

Melissa is a dental assistant in Dr. Clements' office. Mr. Summers is sitting in the dental chair waiting to be prepped for a crown. When Melissa was getting the needle ready for the dentist to numb the area, she noticed that he was quickly becoming unglued. He began to hyperventilate and the look of panic on his face told Melissa that he was on the verge of freaking out. Melissa immediately put down the needle and walked over to Mr. Summers, who was now sitting upright in the chair.

Employee: *"Mr. Summers, I understand that this can be scary. Is this the first crown you've had done?"* **(courtesy, empathy)**

Freaking Out Patient: "Yes! I can't do this!"

Employee: *"It's understandable that you're feeling anxious. Let me assure you, you're not going to feel anything during the procedure. Dr. Clements will need to numb the area first, and then it'll* take only about forty-five minutes to prep the tooth and fit you with a temporary crown. Then we'll be done. *You aren't going to feel any pain or discomfort."* **(rapport, empathy, assurance)**

Patient: "I can't sit through all this. I need to get out of here now!"

Employee: "*Mr. Summers, I understand how you're feeling. Please* take a deep breath. *It's going to be all right. Many of our patients like to listen to soft music during procedures. It'll help you keep your mind focused on something else.* Would you like to try that? I have headphones right here." **(courtesy, empathy, courtesy, assurance, rapport)**

Patient: "No! I just can't go through with this."

Employee: "The reason we scheduled the procedure today is that your tooth is cracked, and we want to get a crown on before the tooth breaks completely. If that were to happen you'd be in an awful lot of pain, and we'd still have to do the crown. *I assure you you're not going to feel anything.* You can close your eyes, listen to the music, *and we'll be done before you know. I promise."* **(assurance)**

> (Melissa made eye contact as she spoke assertively, and when she was finished she smiled sympathetically. She noticed Mr. Summers take a deep breath and he appeared to calm a bit.)

Employee: "*I had to have one done last year so I'm speaking from experience and I can relate to how you're feeling. It'll be fine."* **(rapport, empathy, assurance)**

Patient: "Okay. I know you're right. I need to get it done. I think I'll try listening to music."

Employee: "*Great!* Now just close your eyes and continue breathing deeply and slowly. *That always helps me stay calm."* **(enthusiasm, rapport)**

Why This Works

Melissa recognized immediately that Mr. Summers was quickly losing control of his emotions and, when he began acting irrationally, she stopped what she was doing, walked over to him, and spoke in a reassuring voice. The first words out of her mouth formed a phrase of empathy, followed by a phrase of assurance, and she continued to use these types of phrases throughout her conversation. In addition, she worked on building a rapport with the patient. She did not become unnerved by his behavior, but remained calm, which helped him calm down. Melissa made eye contact and spoke in a controlled, soft tone of voice, taking the time to explain the procedure and how long it would take. Consequently, her logical explanation and caring words and actions helped him return to a rational state.

Applying the Approach

When handling a customer who is freaking out, apply the following principles to your situations:

- Stop what you're doing, and immediately deal with the behavior.
- Take a deep breath! This will help you stay calm when a person is losing it.
- Your main goal is to calm the person down, but don't say the words, "calm down," as that often upsets an already upset person even more.
- Rather, ask the person to take some deep breaths.
- Rely on phrases of empathy and assurance to convey that you understand what the customer or patient is going through and state exactly what you are going to do and when.
- Be kind and speak in a reassuring, soft tone of voice.

- You need to be the voice of reason, and you're the expert so speak confidently and authoritatively when explaining the procedure.
- Explain exactly what you're going to do and, if appropriate, how long it's going to take.
- Look directly at the person as you speak.
- Maintain a caring facial expression and a relaxed demeanor.
- Smile sympathetically to convey that you understand.
- Pay attention, and when you see that the customer is calming down and returning to rational behavior, gain agreement before proceeding with the interaction.

What to Do When the Customer Is Grumbling

Grumblers are complainers, but they don't complain in the usual sense. When a customer voices a complaint, you listen, ask questions to better understand their problem, and then handle their grievance using powerful phrases and working through the six steps to find a satisfactory solution. Grumblers, on the other hand, complain in a passive-aggressive manner, often using a subtle or backhanded approach, such as muttering under their breath. You can hear the grumbling, but you can't hear what the grumbling is about. People who grumble can be tiresome. Their behavior can be draining. You're doing everything you can to find the best solution to their problem, but when they start to grumble you have to stop and figure out what they're saying. Grumblers may also be disappointed by the solution you've proposed and turn their disappointment into verbal grumbling, or they may simply be grouchy people who grumble about everything.

When a customer starts to grumble, it's disconcerting and distracting. You may have thought you were on the right track, working to find the best solution, only to become confused when the grumbling begins. You don't understand what they're saying. Are they dissatisfied with the solution you proposed? Are you taking too long? Is it your personality? Or does it even have anything to do with you at all? You can lose your focus and may even get derailed by the grumbling.

The best way to handle a grumbler is to deal with the behavior head on so you can get to the root of the issue. Offer a phrase of regret, followed by a phrase of courtesy, such as *'I'm sorry. I didn't hear what you said."* Listen to the customer's response. Perhaps he didn't know how to articulate his complaint. Offer phrases of empathy and assurance: *"I understand. Friday is our first open date. Is that all right?"*

Or she may be passive aggressive and not want to vocalize her complaint: "It's not important." Ask another question to make sure you understood the request correctly: *"Are you sure it's not important? I wasn't able to hear what you said and I want you to be happy with the solution."* "It's okay." Then offer a phrase of assurance: *"Friday is our first open date. Does that work for you?"* In a situation such as this, in which the customer doesn't offer more information, move on through the next steps of the interaction, paying attention to their mood and body language.

Identifying the Behavior

A grumbling customer may:

- Not be an effective communicator.
- Not know how to effectively complain, even when a complaint is valid.
- Like to complain, even when a complaint isn't valid.
- Be grouchy.
- Be surly.
- Talk under his or her breath.
- Mutter in an unintelligible manner.
- Display passive aggressive behavior, such as complaining quietly.
- Be disappointed by the solution and mutter in discontent.
- Look for things to go wrong.

Do This!

Jennifer works for a computer service and repair company. She answers phones, schedules appointments, and prepares invoices. She understands that computers are her customers' lifelines and when the machine breaks down, they need them fixed fast. She answered the following call.

Employee: "World Computers, good morning. My name is Jennifer. How may I help you?" **(welcome)**

Grumbling Customer: "Good morning. This is Paul Woods. I need help, and I need it fast. My computer crashed this morning, and I need you to send someone out."

Employee: "Ouch! That's never good, is it? I'll be happy to schedule an appointment for you. Other than that, how are you doing today?" **(empathy, enthusiasm, rapport)**

Customer: "Other than that, I'm doing great. How soon can you send a tech out?"

Employee: "I'm going to check on that right away. First, I'll need to know what's happening with the computer." **(assurance)**

Customer: "Yesterday it was really slow. Today, when I tried signing on to my email account, I kept getting an error message saying I need to supply my password. I've never had to do that before."

Employee: "And what about your browser? Can you navigate online?"

Customer: "I can, but it takes forever."

Employee: "Hmm, from what you told me about the password and how slow the computer is, it sounds like you might have a virus. The soonest I can schedule a tech to come out is Thursday. I can have someone out between two and four pm. How does that sound?" **(assurance)**

(Jennifer heard Mr. Woods mutter something but she couldn't make out what he said.)

Employee: "I'm sorry, Mr. Woods. I didn't hear what you said." **(regret, courtesy)**

Customer: "It's nothing."

Employee: "I wish I could schedule someone earlier, but Thursday afternoon is the earliest I have open. Is that all right?" **(empathy, assurance)**

(Jennifer again heard grumbling.)

Employee: *"Mr. Woods, I understand your computer is important to you. I've scheduled you between two and four on Thursday. Does that timeframe work for you?"* **(courtesy, assurance)**

Customer: "I guess it'll have to. I use my computer for my business, and it'll be really tough not being able to get into my email for that long."

Employee: *"Oh, I understand. You asked to have a tech come out but I can offer you another option since you use the computer for business. Would you be willing to bring the hard drive in today? If you can do that, my inside tech can work on it for you. Most likely we can get it fixed later today or tomorrow at the latest. How does that sound?"* **(empathy, assurance)**

Customer: "That sounds great. I'll bring it right over."

Why This Works

Jennifer was handling this contact the same way she handled all of her contacts, speaking professionally and interjecting phrases of courtesy, enthusiasm, empathy, and assurance into her conversation. She understood how important computers are to her customers and, when Mr. Woods started grumbling, she addressed his unintelligible muttering immediately. When he said it was nothing, Jennifer sensed by his grumbling that it was indeed something and most likely it was about the delay in sending a tech out. She went a step further and asked him if he was certain the appointment was satisfactory. That's when he opened up and said he used his computer for his business and couldn't operate without it. Jennifer offered an alternative solution, and Mr. Woods was very pleased. In this scenario, Mr. Woods' grumbling arose out of his inability to effectively communicate his displeasure with the initially scheduled date. Because Jennifer was tuned in to the conversation, she was able to uncover the reason for the grumbling and offer him another solution.

Applying the Approach

When handling a customer who is grumbling, apply the following principles to your situations:

- You're likely to encounter grumbling when you're in Step 4, Assisting the Customer. You understood the customer's request and offered your best solution.

- Then you hear grumbling. You don't know the reason for the grumbling—is the customer grouchy by nature, does he have trouble articulating his valid complaint, or does she just like to complain?

- Offer phrases of regret and courtesy to try to get the customer to open up and explain: *"I'm sorry. I wasn't able to hear what you said."*

- If the customer states the reason for the complaint, "I really wanted it in green," you can address the objection to your proposed solution by offering phrases of empathy and assurance: *"I know how it is when you have your heart set on a certain color. It's out of stock now, but let me check on the availability of green and see how soon we can order that color for you."*

- If the customer doesn't open up, try again by asking a question to ensure you understand: "I'm placing the order for that in yellow. Are you sure that'll work for you?"

- If the customer still doesn't open up or continues to mutter, try again. Offer a phrase of empathy followed by a phrase of assurance: *"It seems that might not be acceptable to you. That's the best I can do."*

- After the second attempt, the customer may or may not voice the reason for grumbling. If he or she does, try to find an alternate solution, as Jennifer did with Mr. Woods. If, however, the customer doesn't open up, then at least you can assure yourself that you tried your best. After all, you're not a mind reader.

What to Do When the Customer Is Harassing You

Harassment can be identified as a repeated offensive or highly aggressive behavior toward another that's done for the purpose making the person feel uncomfortable, upset, or scared. When people harass, they're doing it to wear the other person down to agree or comply with them. A customer may bully you if you haven't offered the desired solution. You may have had a friendly conversation with a customer who misinterprets and begins to sexually harass you. Taken to the extreme, some harassers are stalkers who are disturbed or delusional and do not see their behavior as wrong. And, some people may not realize their behavior crossed the line and will immediately stop when you confront the behavior.

Harassing behavior is never acceptable. Repeat: Never acceptable! But it can happen, and it can happen between a customer and an employee. If a customer repeatedly acts out in a manner that makes you feel upset, uncomfortable, or scared, take action immediately. Harassment, unless dealt with, won't stop. First, assume the person doesn't realize the behavior is harassing. Then let the person know, assertively, that his or her behavior makes you uncomfortable and needs to stop. If the customer apologizes and stops the behavior, continue your interaction. If the harassing doesn't stop, involve your boss. And if someone stalks you, get your manager or law enforcement to intervene. Never allow anyone to continue harassing you, as the behavior is likely to escalate.

Identifying the Behavior

A harassing customer may:

- Not understand the behavior is harassing.
- Have misinterpreted your conversation.

- Not realize a line has been crossed.
- Be aggressive by nature.
- Be a bully.
- Be used to getting his or her way.
- Not like to take no for an answer.
- Hope to wear you down so that you will agree or comply.

Do This!

Teri is a personal fitness trainer at a health club. She's friendly and outgoing by nature and, consequently, she's had to learn how to handle clients who ask her out. Her usual response is that she is happily engaged and that has always worked. Recently she began to notice that one of the members of the health club, Eric, has been staring at her during her sessions with her clients and lingers to talk to her. He asked her out once and she told him she was engaged, but today he's staring at her and started working out on the machine next to the one she's working on with a client.

Harassing Customer: "Hey Teri, looks like you're doing a great job."

Employee: *"Excuse me a moment, Susan. Hi Eric, how are you doing?"* **(courtesy, welcome)**

Customer: "I'm great, now that I get to see you. How about if we go for a drink after you get off work?"

Employee: *"Thanks for your offer,* but I'm engaged, remember? I mentioned that last time you asked me out for a drink." **(courtesy)**

Customer: "It's just for a drink, that's all. You can still be engaged and go out with a friend for a drink, can't you?"

Employee: *"Eric,* let me put it another way. I never mix business with my personal life, so *no thank you."* **(courtesy)**

(Teri remained calm when she spoke to him, then she and Susan moved to another machine. She kept her eye on

Eric and was relieved when he left. To her surprise, when she got off work, he was waiting outside for her.)

Customer: "How about if we go for that drink now?"

Employee: "Eric, I'm not going for a drink with you."

Customer: "Aww, com'n, I thought we were friends."

Employee: "I'm going to say this once and once only. Your behavior is making me uncomfortable, and I need it to stop."

Customer: "I don't mean to make you feel uncomfortable. I didn't mean anything by it."

Employee: "Good."

> (Teri felt vulnerable, so she walked back inside the health club and asked one of the male employees to walk her to her car. As they walked outside, Eric made a quick exit and never bothered her again.)

Why This Works

Teri tried handling Eric's behavior by being firm, yet friendly. When that didn't work, she realized he had crossed the line, mistaking her friendly nature, so she assertively and adamantly told him no thanks. She never showed she was upset by his repeated advances, but when he was waiting outside for her she felt uncomfortable and a little scared. She remained calm, clearly stated how his behavior made her feel, and told him she needed him to stop. Then, because she was outside with no other employees around, she did the smart thing by walking back inside the health club and asking another employee to walk her to her car. She also reported the incident to her manager, who spoke to Eric and clearly outlined the steps he'd take if the harassment continued. Consequently, Eric did not bother Teri again.

Applying the Approach

When handling a customer who is harassing, apply the following principles to your situations:

- Harassing behavior, such as bullying, making unwanted sexual advances, or stalking is never to be tolerated. Your safety is more important than trying to provide good customer service when you encounter harassment.
- Your immediate goal is to stop the behavior.
- First, assume the customer doesn't realize the behavior is making you feel uncomfortable, upset, disturbed, or tormented.
- Employ calming techniques: breathe slowly to calm your racing heart, think before you speak, and choose your words carefully.
- Make eye contact, hold your head high, and maintain good posture to signal you are in control.
- Confront the behavior directly, speaking in a controlled tone of voice.
- State that the behavior is making you uncomfortable and you need it stopped.
- Choose a phrase of courtesy, such as, "You're making me uncomfortable. I need you to stop *please.*"
- Listen to the customer's response. If the customer acknowledges and apologizes, move on through your interaction, interjecting phrases of courtesy and enthusiasm: *"Thank you for your apology. I'll be happy to help you now."*
- Unless you feel comfortable after the apology, forego attempts at building a rapport, as that may send a mixed signal to the customer.
- If, however, the customer doesn't acknowledge or apologize and the behavior continues, don't threaten but begin with a phrase of

courtesy and then explain your action: *"Excuse me a moment,* I'm going to get my boss to help me."

- Immediately get your boss or someone in authority to help you handle the customer.

- If the harassment continues, tell your boss and document the incident (or incidents), noting the date, time, occurrence, and any witnesses.

- If, at any time, you feel the situation is becoming dangerous and your safety may be compromised, get law enforcement involved.

What to Do When the Customer Is Impulsive

Have you ever acted without thinking and made a split second decision only later to regret it? Of course you have. We've all done that. A customer who's impulsive may make a decision before you've gathered enough information to fully understand the request. Impulsive people may think they know what they want before you complete the step of understanding their request. They might be the type of people who make rash decisions based on emotions, or what a friend has, or a television commercial promoting a certain product. Customers who act impulsively may also be in a hurry or think that you're asking for or providing more information than needed.

The bottom line is that when customers act impulsively and make decisions based on any of these reasons, you're not sure they're making the best decision for their needs. Your goal is to provide excellent customer service by finding the best solution for each customer, but how do you do that when the customer has already made up his or her mind? The best way to handle an impulsive customer is to try to slow down the interaction. State that you'd like to ask a few questions in order to better understand his or her needs in order to make sure that's the best solution.

Identifying the Behavior

An impulsive customer may:

- Act without thinking.
- Make hasty decisions.
- Make a decision without thinking about consequences.
- Make a decision based on a strong emotional reaction.

- Find too much information annoying.
- Be in a hurry and not have time to think through the decision.
- Be a reactionary type of personality.
- Act out in a jumpy manner with quick, jerky or fidgety movements.

Do This!

Zach works as a sales and customer service associate for a large appliance store. The store carries many different brands, and he prides himself on knowing his products well. He's attended classes on some of the brands and for others he's read training manuals. His goal is to fit the best appliance for each customer based on their needs.

Employee: *"Good afternoon. My name is Zach. How can I help you?"* **(welcome)**

Impulsive Customer: "Hi Zach, I saw the ad in the paper for the washer and dryer you have on sale. I'd like to buy that set."

(The set on sale wasn't a good value for the money. The machines were cheaply constructed and didn't have a great efficiency rating. He didn't want to finalize the deal with the customer until he asked some questions.)

Employee: *"Great, I'll be glad to help you. May I have your name, please?"* **(enthusiasm, courtesy)**

Customer: "It's Sandy. Sandy Daniels."

Employee: *"Thanks, Sandy.* I'm familiar with the set we have on sale but before you settle on that, *would it be all right* if I ask you a few questions to make sure it's the best set for your needs?" **(courtesy)**

Customer: "This is the one I saw, it's on sale, and that's the set I want."

Employee: *"I certainly understand where you're coming from.* The reason I'd like to ask you some questions is that we have other sets that don't cost much more than the advertised special. I feel they're more durable, have more options, and you may decide you'd prefer one of those sets." **(empathy)**

Customer: "I came in here knowing what I want and what I want to spend. This fits into my budget so I'll just take that set. I mean, a washer's a washer right?"

Employee: "Well, actually they aren't all created equally. *I can assure you, it won't take me long. I'd like to find out how much use the washer will get and then I'll be able to compare the sale set with some of the others. Believe me, we have others that are made better, and I'm confident they'll fit into your budget."* **(assurance)**

Customer: "Well, all right. I just don't want to be raked over the coals."

Employee: "I understand. *I wouldn't do that to you, and thanks for giving me the opportunity.* Now, can you tell me what your washing habits are?" **(empathy, rapport, courtesy)**

Why This Works

Zach knew the set his company ran in the current sale flyer wasn't made well. When Sandy told him that's the set she wanted, he could have sold it to her and pocketed his commission. But his goal was to make sure he found the best product for her needs and, because she had mentioned cost was a factor, to find it at around the same price. He was polite and offered phrases of empathy, courtesy, and assurance to get Sandy on his side. He didn't know the reason for her impulsiveness but in the event that it was because she was in a hurry, he assured her it wouldn't take that long for him to understand her needs and compare some other sets to the one she asked for. When she said she didn't want to be taken advantage of, he empathized and established a rapport by saying he wouldn't do that. He was able to get her on his side and moved the interaction forward to understand her needs.

Applying the Approach

When handling a customer who is impulsive, apply the following principles to your situations:

- If what the customer asks for is the best solution or the only solution, then it may be best to complete the transaction without moving through the understanding step of the interaction.

- If this is the case, you'll want to ask a question to gain agreement, such as, "You're ordering the water filter model number 449273. I've got a picture of it on my screen. Do you want to look at it to make sure it's the same one you have?"

- If there are options, however, you'll want to make sure that what the customer is asking for is indeed the best solution. You'll need to get the customer on your side so that you can ask some questions.

- Choose phrases of enthusiasm, courtesy, empathy, and rapport to gain the customer's trust: *"I'll be happy to help. Before I ring up the sale, I'd like to ask a couple questions, please. I understand you asked for that, but I may have another product that'll better suit your needs."*

- Phrases of assurance can also get the customer on your side: *"This won't take long. I'll make sure of that."*

- Tune in to the customer completely. Tune out all distractions. Listen to what the customer says and pay attention to the body language.

- Maintain a positive attitude by being interested, helpful, and enthusiastic.

- When you gain the customer's agreement to ask questions, be efficient and stop asking when you have enough information.

- Then assist the customer by recommending the best solution.

- Say why you feel this solution is better than what the customer asked for.
- Assure the customer he or she is making a good decision.
- If, however, you can't gain the customer's agreement to ask questions, complete the interaction based on what the customer wants. Politely state that you wish you had the opportunity to make sure that's the best solution and offer a phrase of appreciation to validate the customer's choice.

What to Do When the Customer Is Indecisive

Customers who are indecisive are most likely not only indecisive in their dealing with you; they can't make up their minds about anything. They'll waver back and forth, and when you think they're close to finalizing a decision, the wavering will begin again. Indecisive people may take a couple minutes to make up their minds or the wishy-washy behavior may continue until you feel like pulling your hair out. But you don't pull your hair out. You wait. And wait. And hope they'll make up their minds already!

Handling customers who can't make decisions can be mind boggling. They waver back and forth, and when they begin the "yes, no, I don't know," you may have the urge to shake them and say, "Just make up your mind, will you?" Then you bite your tongue and wait with them. The good news is that you can help an indecisive customer make up his or her mind. Establishing a rapport and relying on phrases of enthusiasm and assurance will help you throughout these contacts. When you've established a rapport and the customer trusts you and is on your side, review the options and explain the pros and cons of each. If that doesn't work, it can be helpful to walk the customer through the decision by using a process of elimination until you're down to one choice. Then quickly move into the agreement step, assure the customer the decision is a good one, acknowledge the decision, and end the interaction.

Identifying the Behavior

An indecisive customer may:

- Act in a hesitant manner.
- Waver back and forth.

- Be wishy-washy.
- Be overly picky.
- Not be able to make a decision.
- Flip flop between yes, no, maybe, and I don't know.
- Look back and forth between the products several times.
- Scratch their heads or have a bewildered facial expression.
- Have too many choices and become confused.
- Be trying to decide between very similar choices.
- Feel anxious about spending a large amount of money on the product.

Do This!

Christine is an interior decorator, so she's used to dealing with clients who can't make up their minds. Through experience, she's learned to identify these customers and has developed her personal "tool kit" for helping them, which includes her proven methods to move them through the decision process. She's currently working with a customer, who's selecting colors for her new home. One of the first things Christine did when she met this client was to build a rapport and establish trust, and she's on a first name basis with Rachel.

Employee: "Hi Rachel, thanks for coming in today. How is the home coming along?" **(welcome, courtesy, rapport)**

Indecisive Customer: "Hi Christine, I'm so flustered! The contractor seems to be dragging his feet. I'm afraid he's going to get behind schedule."

Employee: "Oh Boy, I can relate to how you're feeling. Sometimes it seems as though they're getting behind but I know this builder and he's very reliable." **(empathy, rapport)**

Customer: "I hope so."

Employee: "He assured me he's on schedule so I wouldn't worry *about it.* Today we need to finalize the interior colors. Once that's done, we can start selecting the furniture and fabrics. *I'm so excited that we're at this point already.* Last time you were here, I sent home some of the paint swatches you selected. Have you decided on the colors for each room?" **(assurance, rapport, enthusiasm)**

Customer: "I'm afraid I can't decide. I don't know, maybe there's some other colors I didn't take home that I'd like better. I just don't want to make the wrong choice and be sorry."

> (Christine was afraid of this. Rachel had been indecisive about every decision up to this point and even selecting the color palette had taken forever. Now it's crucial that she finalize the paint choices because the builder said he'll be ready to begin the interior painting in a couple days.)

Employee: "*I know how difficult that can be. I'm confident that because we took so much time choosing the color palette that you made the right decisions about the colors. Here's what I've done in the past, and it works well.* I'm going to lay out all the colors you chose and unless something pops out at you, we'll work in reverse, starting with your least favorite for each room. Let's start with the great room. *I absolutely guarantee this process works, and I'm certain that you'll make the right choices.*" **(empathy, rapport, assurance, enthusiasm)**

Customer: "Christine, I trust you completely. That sounds good."

Why This Works

Because Christine had already established a rapport with her, Rachel trusted and accepted her advice. When she became indecisive about the colors previously selected, Christine knew it was important to reinforce that decision, otherwise they'd be back to square one. She didn't offer more choices, nor did she try to make up Rachel's mind for her, but rather laid out a plan whereby they would work through a process of elimination. She interjected phrases of empathy, enthusiasm, rapport, and assurance, and projected a great attitude throughout the contact. After Rachel makes the final choices, Christine plans to quickly move to the agreement and acknowledge steps to successfully end this interaction.

Applying the Approach

When handling a customer who is indecisive, apply the following principles to your situations:

- You'll likely notice the indecision when you are in the assisting step.

- Further the rapport you have been building with the indecisive customer to foster the trusting relationship you've built.

- The customer's facial expression and body language may clue you in to feelings of indecision. The customer may not vocalize the indecision but rather look confused or keep going back and forth looking at or picking up each product.

- Acknowledge the indecision by offering a phrase of empathy: *"I know it can be hard to choose."*

- Choose phrases of enthusiasm and assurance as you walk the customer through the decision: *"and I'm positive that you'll make the right choice. I'm here to help you do that."*

- It might help to ask more questions: "Which one are you leaning toward?" or "What questions do you have?"

- When you offer the options, explain the pros of cons of each.

- If possible, when offering your solution, try to limit the choices, as too many can be overwhelming.

- As Christine did, using the process of elimination can be a helpful tool.

- Don't try to put words in the customer's mouth or make up his or her mind.

- Offer reassurance when you feel the person is nearing a decision.

- When the customer signals the decision, quickly move through the agreement step into the acknowledgement step.

- Reinforce the decision by offering a phrase of appreciation: *"You made a great choice. I know you'll be happy with it."*

- Maintain a positive attitude throughout what can be a very taxing interaction and keep your facial expressions friendly.

What to Do When the Customer Is Intoxicated

It's pretty easy to tell when someone is drunk. Even if you never saw the person before, you can usually tell by someone's appearance and speech. If you suspect the person is drunk, pay close attention to the way her or she acts. Glazed or half-closed eyes are a good sign someone has had too much to drink. People who are drunk will have slurred speech and may find inappropriate things funny or amusing. When they stand, they are likely to sway back and forth, be unable to walk normally, and may even need assistance walking. For simplicity purposes, we're focusing on intoxication in this section; however, this type of behavior is also displayed by people who are high or who may be having a reaction to medicines.

If you encounter someone who's intoxicated, or high, or having a drug reaction, it's imperative that you act ethically and not contribute to the problem, especially if you work in the food and beverage industry. Serving alcohol to someone who's displaying this type of behavior may cost you your job, result in a heavy fine for your business owner, a loss of the liquor license, or, worst case scenario, it may cost a life. Even if you don't work in a restaurant or bar, you may encounter an intoxicated person who stumbles upon your place of business. If that happens, by no means should you ignore this behavior in any public place, as this person is likely to get into a vehicle and drive, so get your boss to help you deal with him or her.

Identifying the Behavior

An intoxicated customer may:

- Have impaired speech, balance, and coordination.
- Have glazed, bloodshot, or half-closed eyes.

- Slur words.
- Be unable to communicate logically.
- Speak incoherently.
- Speak loudly.
- Find inappropriate things funny or amusing.
- Speak to strangers as though they are friends.
- Become belligerent when his or her condition is addressed.
- Sway back and forth or reel when standing.
- Stumble or have trouble walking.

Do This!

Angela is a server in an upscale restaurant. She is a people person and enjoys her job because she gets to meet a variety of people. Tonight, a couple at one of her tables appears to be intoxicated. She served them two drinks, but by the way they're behaving, she suspects they had been drinking before they came in. She's paying close attention to their behavior and when the man ordered another round, he looked at her with glassy eyes, slurred his words, and his companion laughed giddily when he didn't order properly.

Intoxicated Customer: "We'wl haf two more . . . les see . . . wha di we haf?"

Employee: *"Sir,* I think you'd better wait a while before you have another round. *I'll be happy to get your dinner order in,* and then let's see how you feel, okay?" **(courtesy, enthusiasm)**

Customer: "I fil fine. Jush get us one more, den we'll order."

Employee: *"Look, I understand you're out and you want to have a good time. I like to have a good time too.* But if I were to keep serving you alcohol, I could lose my job or you could get hurt, and I'm not willing to do that. *So right now let's get you something to eat."* **(empathy, rapport, assurance)**

Customer: "Are you callin me drunk? I'm fine."

(Angela now felt certain the man was intoxicated. Besides the glassy eyes and slurring his words, he spoke a little too loudly.)

Employee: "*Sir,* I haven't called you anything. But it appears, by the way you're acting, that you've had a little too much to drink. *I'm not serving you any more liquor.* If you'd like, I'll call my manager over." **(courtesy, assurance)**

Customer: "No, no, no. Iss all right. We'll eat."

Employee: "*Great! What can I get for you?*" **(enthusiasm)**

Why This Works

Because Angela paid close attention, she quickly identified that this customer and his companion were intoxicated. She held her ground; was firm, yet respectful, in the way she spoke to the man; and did not back down on her refusal when he requested one more round. Her tone was authoritative, and she demonstrated that she was the one in charge. Angela acted ethically and did the right thing. By doing so, she did not contribute to the problem.

Applying the Approach

When handling a customer who is intoxicated, apply the following principles to your situations:

- Before addressing the issue of intoxication, pay attention to the customer's behavior to make sure your hunch is correct. If you observe some or all of the behaviors listed above, assume the person has had too much to drink (or is high).

- Handle the situation ethically: Never serve more liquor to a person who is intoxicated.

- If the person has been drinking, assertively speak up and explain to the customer that it appears he or she has had a little too much and you're not going to serve another drink.

- If you haven't served liquor, the behavior could have been caused by a reaction to drugs so tread lightly when approaching the subject. Focus on the exhibited behaviors rather than assuming it's because of drinking. For example, say "I notice that you're having trouble with your balance. Would you like to sit down?"

- Speak quietly and respectfully to maintain the dignity of the customer.

- Don't embarrass the person, especially in front of other people.

- Speak in a friendly, calm voice.

- Don't argue with someone who's drunk.

- If the person persists, explain that it's against the policy of the business.

- If the person becomes belligerent after you've tried unsuccessfully to reason with him or her, involve your manager.

- Keep in mind that if you ask the person to leave your place of business, you're responsible for his or her safety, as well as the safety of others, so if need be, get the police or a security guard involved.

What to Do When the Customer Is Melodramatic

Some people love to play to an audience, and that includes customers whose audience is you and other customers. Melodramatic people like to exaggerate and may emote, speaking loudly, and enunciate their words. Some customers are naturally attention seekers and may be looking for reassurance, while others thrive on conflict, as that gives them their stage. They like to enhance the problem or cause of the conflict. Displaying melodramatic behavior puts them center stage. The bottom line is that when a customer behaves this way, he or she is doing it to garner attention, and the attention can be either for a negative or a positive reason.

Melodramatic behavior can be amusing, but if it's overdone or taken to extremes, it can be downright annoying both to you and other customers. The bad news is that this behavior may prove so bothersome to other customers that they decide to leave your place of business rather than get caught up in the drama. The good news is that you can turn around melodramatic behavior without becoming melodramatic yourself. If you're dealing with someone who's an attention seeker or looking for reassurance or a compliment, offer phrases of enthusiasm and appreciation: *"I like it! You made a great decision, and I know you'll be happy with that."* If the customer is dramatizing a complaint, a phrase of regret, followed by phrases of empathy and assurance, can help: *"I'm very sorry. I'd feel the same way if that happened to me, and I'm going to take care of it for you."* It can also help to offer a phrase of rapport, as melodramatic types often seek recognition. In any event, the best way to handle someone who is melodramatic is to not play to his or her audience, but rather offer a powerful phrase or two, and move on.

Identifying the Behavior

A melodramatic customer may:

- Be highly excitable.
- Be highly emotional.
- Add drama to everything.
- Overreact.
- Love attention.
- Like to play to an audience.
- Thrive on conflict as it gives them a stage.
- Display exaggerated gestures.
- Speak loudly and emotively.
- Come across in an insincere manner.

Do This!

Heather is a receptionist in a day spa. Her responsibilities include making appointments for clients, checking them in, and making sure they're comfortable if they have to wait. When Heather saw Ms. Boone walk in, she wondered why the client arrived thirty minutes early for her appointment. The masseuse is with another client, and Ms. Boone is going to have a long wait.

Employee: *"Hi Ms. Boone. You look so pretty today. That shade of blue is a great color for you."* (**welcome, rapport**)

Melodramatic Customer: *"Well, thank you, Heather! You're so kind."*

Employee: *"You're welcome.* Bonnie is about halfway through with her client so *please* have a seat, and *I'll be happy to get you something to drink while you wait."* (**courtesy, enthusiasm**)

(Heather noticed Ms. Boone look around the room at the two other women who were waiting. Ms. Boone then leaned into her and spoke in a loud whisper, making sure the others could hear.)

Customer: "I came in early because I wanted to speak to you first. Last time I was here I didn't like the way Bonnie treated me. She was pretty rough and my back hurt for two days. Two days!"

(Ms. Boone looked around the room as she said the second "Two Days!" The women who were waiting both looked up from the magazines they were reading.)

Customer: "I don't know if Bonnie was angry or upset about something but she certainly seemed to take her aggression out on me! I'm thinking that maybe I'd like to try the other masseuse today."

Employee: *"I'm so sorry that happened. I can understand your feelings. Why don't I speak to Bonnie first and I'll make sure that doesn't happen again."* **(regret, empathy, assurance)**

Customer: "I don't know. What do you ladies think? I mean, if your back hurt for two days afterward would you try that person again?"

(One of the women shrugged her shoulders. The other had buried herself in the magazine.)

Employee: *"You've been seeing Bonnie for a long time and since it's never happened before, I give you my assurance that we won't let it happen again. I'll speak to Bonnie before you see her. I know that she enjoys you, as do I, and we both appreciate your business."* **(rapport, assurance, appreciation)**

Customer: "Well thank you! I enjoy you and Bonnie too. As long as you speak to her, that'll be fine."

Employee: *"You're welcome. Of course I will. I'm so happy that we can work this out for you. Now, may I get you something to drink while you wait?"* **(courtesy, assurance, enthusiasm, courtesy)**

Why This Works

Heather knew this client to be melodramatic, someone who craved attention, so she made sure that she offered a phrase of rapport every time Ms. Boone came in. But this time Ms. Boone had a complaint that Heather had to deal with. When Ms. Boone addressed the other ladies who were waiting, Heather did not play to the audience or involve them. She didn't raise her voice or mimic Ms. Boone's emotive style, but rather spoke in a calm voice using a helpful, concerned tone. She addressed the complaint, kept her attention on Ms. Boone, and was able to resolve the issue quickly and satisfactorily. She suspects that drama will always surround Ms. Boone, yet she is also confident that by continually working on building a rapport with her, she'll be able to handle the melodramatic behavior to the best of her ability.

Quick Tip for a Sticky Situation

If the melodrama continues after you've offered phrases of rapport, empathy, and/or assurance, and the customer still wants to play to an audience, think about the motive. If the customer is an attention seeker and harmless, ignore the melodrama and continue through your interaction. If, however, the customer is a complainer who continues to loudly complain to other customers after you've offered a valid solution, try to separate him or her from the crowd. If you have a quiet place to speak, politely say, "Let's go over here so we can talk without the other customers hearing us." Usually melodramatic types are people who just want to be heard, so removing the audience can often quiet the melodrama.

Applying the Approach

When handling a customer who is melodramatic, apply the following principles to your situations:

- Don't react to someone who is overreacting.
- Stay calm, pay attention, and listen for the reason behind the melodrama.
- Don't play to the audience, but rather keep your focus on dealing with the customer's behavior and completing the interaction.
- Maintain a friendly facial expression and a relaxed demeanor.
- When a person craves attention, establishing a rapport will often provide the needed attention.
- Offer phrases of rapport and empathy: *"The same thing happened to me yesterday. I know exactly how you feel."*
- Some customers thrive on complaining, as that gives them their stage. The complaint may or may not even be valid. These people look for things to go wrong.
- If the person is melodramatic when voicing a complaint, immediately offer phrases of regret and assurance: *"I apologize that happened. I'm going to get to the bottom of this right now and make it right for you."*
- Whatever you do, remain in control. Speak softly and speak only to the melodramatic customer, not the other customers who may be listening.
- As quickly as you can, move through the six steps of the interaction, handling the melodramatic customer efficiently and ensuring satisfaction before offering a phrase of appreciation: *"I'm glad I could help you today. Thanks for coming in."*

What to Do When the Customer Is Mentally Unstable

You may not recognize mentally unstable behavior immediately. People who are mentally unstable can be unpredictable. They may be calm one minute and fly off the handle the next. They have difficulty coping and may react to a word you say or an action you take. Their behavior may fluctuate wildly when they're unable to control their emotions. Mentally unstable people may be on medications that either control the behavior or exacerbate it. This is one of the toughest and touchiest types of behavior you'll encounter because anything you say or do might trigger bad or dangerous behavior.

If the customer begins acting erratically and you suspect it's due to mental illness, pay close attention. Try to get through the interaction without pushing the customer's buttons. The best way to handle someone who's mentally unstable is to stay calm and speak in a controlled voice using phrases of courtesy and assurance: *"Sir, I'm going to help you right now."* Don't try to build a rapport as your friendliness may be misread. Be careful when offering a phrase of empathy, such as *"I know how you feel."* You might unwittingly unhinge an unstable person, who may angrily respond, "You have no idea how I feel!" As long as the customer remains calm, get through the interaction by staying professional and focusing on handling the request. Listen carefully to make sure you understand the customer and also to watch for any deterioration in behavior. Project a positive attitude, stay composed, maintain a neutral facial expression, and a relaxed demeanor.

Your safety is paramount. If you see any signs of anger, aggression, or erratic behavior that is spiraling downward get help immediately. Someone who's unstable may be calm one moment, aggressive the next, and turn violent in a heartbeat. Don't panic if you suspect mental instability, but get help any time you feel you need it. Even if you're a trained health professional, don't solely try to handle an aggressive mentally unstable person who begins acting out.

Identifying the Behavior

A mentally unstable customer may:

- Have varying degrees of mental instability.
- Have difficulty coping.
- Not be able to control emotions.
- Be unpredictable.
- Act erratically.
- React to certain words and actions.
- Have wildly fluctuating behavior.
- Be calm one moment and upset or angry with no provocation.
- Suddenly become unreasonable.
- Display physical signs such as shifty eyes, excessive blinking, sweating, or jumpy movements.
- Be on medications that distort personality.

Do This!

Mindy is a receptionist in a law office. One of her responsibilities is to greet clients and notify the attorneys when a client is waiting. Mr. Perry just walked into the office and, although one of the attorneys is actively handling a wrongful termination suit for him, he did not have an appointment scheduled today. Mindy felt uncomfortable whenever he came in, but especially today, since he had no appointment. Because of past behaviors she's observed, she suspects he's mentally unstable.

Employee: *"Good Morning, Mr. Perry. How can I help you?"* **(welcome, courtesy)**

Mentally Unstable Client: "Hi. I want to see Ms. Watkins."

Employee: *I'll be happy to let her know you're here.* I don't have an appointment noted for you for today, though. Is she expecting you?" **(enthusiasm)**

Client: "No. What's the problem?"

Employee: *"Mr. Perry, there's no problem. I'll let Ms. Watkins know you're waiting.* She's with another client right now and their meeting just started, so I'm not sure how soon she can see you." **(courtesy, assurance)**

Client: "She told me to come in and see her anytime. How long is it going to be? I don't have all day. I'm in a hurry, and I just need to ask her something."

(Mindy became concerned by Mr. Perry's immediate change in behavior. He had been calm when he came in but as soon as she mentioned the attorney was with another client, he became agitated. When he said that Ms. Watkins told him to come in anytime rather than schedule appointments as was the norm, Mindy felt certain that her suspicions about his mental instability were correct.)

Employee: *"All right, Mr. Perry. Please excuse me a moment, and I'll check right now to see how soon she can see you. Please have a seat."* **(courtesy, assurance, courtesy)**

(Mr. Perry started pacing back and forth, running his hand through his hair. It was clear to Mindy that his behavior was deteriorating. After excusing herself, she spoke to Ms. Watkins and also to one of the partners before she returned to the front office.)

Employee: *"Ms. Watkins assured me she'll be able to see you shortly. I'd like to introduce you to Mr. Randolph, one of the partners in our firm."* **(assurance, courtesy)**

(Mr. Perry glared at Mr. Randolph and said nothing.)

Partner: *"Mr. Perry, it's good to meet you. I understand from Mindy that you need to see your attorney but that you're in a hurry. Ms. Watkins will be finished with her client in about ten minutes. She asked me to see if I can help you in any way so you won't have to wait."* **(courtesy, welcome, assurance)**

Client: "Um, no. I'll wait. It's okay."

(Mr. Perry took a seat and appeared to be more in control of his emotions. Just to be on the safe side, Mr. Randolph lingered by Mindy's desk feigning interest in something on her computer. When he sensed that Mr. Perry was staying calm, he went back to his office, but he planned to make his presence known when Ms. Watkins met with Mr. Perry.)

Why This Works

Mindy became uncomfortable when Mr. Perry showed up without an appointment, but she stayed calm and spoke courteously, assuring him that Ms. Watkins would see him as soon as she could. When he became a little unglued, she did the right thing by excusing herself and returning with one of the partners. Mindy never showed fear, but rather maintained a professional attitude and spoke in a controlled, soft voice. Mr. Randolph was also nonchalant in his approach when he politely asked if he could help in any way since Mr. Perry had mentioned he was in a hurry. Even though this tactic calmed Mr. Perry, Mr. Randolph planned to stay close by until he left the office.

Applying the Approach

When handling a customer who is mentally unstable, apply the following principles to your situations:

- Stay calm, composed, and controlled.
- Keep a neutral facial expression and maintain a neutral demeanor.

- Project confidence and choose positive words. Keep your conversation limited to handling the customer's request.

- Refrain from attempting to establish a rapport as your friendliness or interest might be misconstrued.

- Speak softly and offer phrases of courtesy and assurance: *"I'll check on this right away. May I have your account number please?"*

- Avoid offering phrases of empathy, such as *"I understand,"* or *"I know just how you feel."* Let's face it: you have no idea how a mentally unstable person feels.

- If a mentally unstable customer shares something personal with you, rather offer a phrase of regret: *"I'm sorry about that."*

- Don't push buttons.

- If you notice a sudden increase in agitation or aggression, pay close attention.

- Stay professional and work through the six steps of the interaction as quickly and efficiently as you can.

- Stop the interaction and get help immediately if you feel your safety is compromised.

What to Do When the Customer Is Noncommunicative

As a frontline employee whose job it is to communicate with customers, handling someone who won't communicate with you can be frustrating. People are noncommunicative for a number of reasons. Your customer may be distrustful of your company because of a negative impression or because you're requesting necessary information they don't want to provide. They may also be shy, standoffish, or an introvert who finds communicating with others difficult, whether in business or personal interactions. Noncommunication may occur as well when there is a generation gap. You might be a Gen-X'er or a Baby Boomer attempting to interact with a Gen-Y'er. You're trying to communicate with a young person who grew up interacting with computers and smart phones. Gen-Y'ers are used to immediacy and may feel more comfortable interacting by text rather than by having a conversation with a person. Whatever the reason for the inability or lack of desire to communicate, dealing with a noncommunicative customer can be extremely difficult if they aren't willing to give you the information you need to handle the request.

When you're trying to communicate with a customer who is noncommunicative, phrases of empathy and assurance can help, such as *"I understand you don't want to share that info, but I'll need it in order to process the claim."* Explaining why you need the information is often helpful since the customer may become more open once he or she understands the reason why you're asking. Trying to establish a rapport and demonstrating that you're ethical can also be helpful to get the customer on your side: *"Before I worked here I wouldn't have understood why our agency needs all this information either. I want you to know that the information you provide is completely private. We never divulge it."* Establishing a rapport and showing that you're ethical can often get a noncommunicative person to open up and engage in a conversation as well. When you're able to do that, the customer is more apt to relax and trust you.

Identifying the Behavior

A noncommunicative customer may:

- Be distrustful.
- Be shy.
- Be standoffish.
- Be aloof.
- Not make eye contact.
- Not show emotion.
- Not engage in a conversation.
- Give one word or short answers that don't fully answer the question.
- Withhold information.
- Refuse to answer questions.
- Tell you he or she doesn't understand why you need the information.

Do This!

Brian works for the county as a building inspector. On the days he's in his office, he also helps customers file new building permits. He deals both with contractors and private homeowners and today he is handling a homeowner, Mr. Harrison, who was noncommunicative from the time Brian greeted him.

Employee: *"Mr. Harrison, are you building an addition on your home?"*
(courtesy)

Noncommunicative Customer: "It's not an addition."

Employee: "You mentioned that you hired a contractor who told you that you'd need a permit. What exactly did you hire him to do?"

Customer: "I don't know why I need a permit. He's just doing a small job for me, not an addition."

Employee: "*I understand.* Since your builder sent you here, the job he's doing for you requires a permit. That's why I asked what you're adding. *I'll need to know that to process the paperwork.*" **(empathy, assurance)**

Customer: "He's just adding on to my deck, that's all."

Employee: "*Great, thank you.* What are the dimensions of the part he's adding?" **(enthusiasm, courtesy)**

Customer: "I don't know. Very small. I really don't understand why I need this permit. It's just a few boards."

Employee: "*Mr. Harrison,* the reason I'm asking you for the dimensions *is I'll need that and some other information in order to pull the permit for you.* The fees vary depending on the type of project and that's why I need the specific details. That's the only way I'll know how to charge you correctly. *I'm here to help you. It's going to be worth the small hassle of pulling a permit when the job's done and you're sitting on that deck enjoying yourself.*" **(courtesy, assurance, rapport)**

Customer: "That kinda puts it in perspective. You're right. I'll be happy when it's all done. I think he said we're extending it ten or twelve feet. I'm not real sure. I didn't know this would be such a hassle."

Employee: "*I know it seems that way, but as I said I'm going to help you get through it as painlessly as possible. Here's what I'm going to do to speed this along.* I'll explain everything I'll need from you in order to pull the permit. You can call me later if you don't have the information with you. We'll need the exact dimensions the contractor is adding, the license number of the contractor. . . ." **(empathy, assurance)**

Why This Works

Working for the government, Brian is used to handling customers who are noncommunicative. But he also needs specific information to process permits, and he's found ways to get customers on his side. When dealing with Mr. Harrison, he interjected phrases of empathy and assurance. Brian conveyed that while he understood Mr. Harrison's reluctance, the information he needed was required. Then he took the time to explain why he needed it. When he tried to establish a rapport, Mr. Harrison let down his guard and began to see Brian as a human being rather than the government, and he began communicating more openly. Brian followed up with another phrase of empathy and assurance and moved on through the interaction.

Quick Tip for a Sticky Situation

If you're a Gen-X'er or a Baby Boomer trying to interact with a Gen-Y customer who's constantly plugged in, prefers to text rather than talk, and used to immediate results, he or she is not likely to be into small talk, so trying to establish a rapport may be fruitless. If you sense this is the reason for the noncommunication, handle the interaction as efficiently as you can without sacrificing the step of asking enough questions to fully understand their request.

Applying the Approach

When handling a customer who is noncommunicative, apply the following principles to your situations:

- Don't take the customer's behavior personally. The reasons may range from shyness to mistrust.
- Offer phrases of empathy and assurance to try to get the customer

on your side: *"I can relate to how you're feeling. I'm going to handle your request but I will need that information to do so."*

- Then explain why you need the information: *"I won't be able to get your claim started until I have all the pertinent details."*

- Try to establish a rapport to get the customer to open up: *"Once I gather the necessary information, the process will move a lot quicker. I was in an accident about a year ago and I got a little frustrated by it all, and I work here!"*

- If you feel it will be beneficial, stress your ethical position: *"These are the same questions we need to ask all customers."*

- Maintain a positive attitude and a calm speaking voice. Display, through your body language and facial expressions, your willingness to help and an understanding of the customer's feelings.

What to Do When the Customer Is Obnoxious

Describing obnoxious behavior is difficult because "obnoxious" has become the catch-all term frontline employees often turn to when describing customers whose behavior is so bad it's the only word that comes to mind. Customers may act obnoxiously for no apparent reason. However, some obnoxious behavior may also be caused by many of the behaviors listed in this chapter, including agitation, condescension, or just being demanding, but obnoxious customers take the behavior to the nth degree. An obnoxious customer may be rude, crass, or downright offensive. It's extreme bad behavior because it's never deserved by the recipient. No one, no matter the circumstances, deserves to be treated in a disrespectful manner. Handling a customer who is obnoxious is likely to leave you flustered or distracted to the point you can't concentrate. These are the customers you're likely to talk about at the lunch or break table, and for lack of a better description you'll blurt out, "I just handled the most obnoxious customer!"

So what's the best way to handle those customers who leave you so flustered or upset you can't think straight? First rule to remember: It's not about you. People who act obnoxiously are likely this way with many others— possibly with everyone. Second rule to remember: Don't take obnoxious behavior personally. And as much as you might be tempted, stay above the fray. Don't mimic an obnoxious customer's tone or the words used. Don't even try to defend yourself: "Sir, I am not a moron." The best advice is to ignore obnoxious behavior as best as you can. Don't let the customer's words get to you. They're only words, after all. Handle the customer as you would any other, using phrases of courtesy and assurance: *"Thank you, I'll put your order in right away."* If a customer is obnoxious about a mistake, offer a phrase of regret, followed by one of assurance: *"I'm sorry your order was misplaced. I'm going to place the order and then I'll speak to my production department to get it expedited."* Don't forget to end the transaction without offering a phrase of appreciation: *"Thank you for your business."* Then let it go. Talking about an obnoxious customer while on break is going to keep your focus on the negative. If someone asks about the contact, just say, "Look, I don't know her situation or what caused her to act that way." Then change the subject.

Identifying the Behavior

An obnoxious customer may:

- Speak loudly.
- Be crass or rude.
- Be overly demanding.
- Be disrespectful.
- Be unable to self-sensor.
- Not care what comes out of his or her mouth.
- Call you or your company by a disrespectful word.
- Disrupt your train of thought.
- Be highly offensive.
- Disagree constantly.
- Play to the audience.
- Be obnoxious to everyone.

Do This!

Amy works for a restaurant that handles both customers who dine in, and who order take out. Today she's working the front counter, handling phone customers placing to go orders as well as customers picking up orders. She was on the phone with a customer, writing down her order, when a man butted in.

Obnoxious Customer: "I've been sitting here ten minutes. When is my order going to be ready?"

Employee to phone customer: *"Excuse me one moment."* **(courtesy)**

Employee: *"Sir, I'm almost finished with my customer. I'll check on your order as soon as I'm done."* **(courtesy, assurance)**

Customer: "No, no, no! I'm not waiting any longer. This is ridiculous. When I called, you told me the order would be ready in twenty minutes. It's been over a half hour already."

Employee: *"I apologize for that. We've been extremely busy. It should be right up, and if not, I'll check as soon as I'm done with this call."* **(regret, assurance)**

> (Amy returned to her call while the obnoxious customer drummed noisily and looked to the other people waiting, speaking to them loudly.)

Customer: "They must have a bunch of idiots working here."

> (Amy hung up the phone and turned to the customer.)

Employee: *"Thank you for waiting. I'll check on your order now. May I have your name please?"* **(courtesy, assurance, courtesy)**

Customer: "Morris."

Employee: *"I'll be right back."* **(assurance)**

Employee: *"Mr. Morris, they're bagging your order right now. I've got the receipt so I can ring you up."* **(assurance)**

Customer: "Ring me up? It should be free! My time is valuable. I'll never come here again."

Employee: *"I'm sorry it took longer than expected. We value your business, and I hope that you'll reconsider."* **(regret, appreciation)**

Customer: "I think you must have a bunch of idiots working in the back. I mean, how hard is it to bag up some chicken and potato salad? This is absurd!"

(Amy handed him his change and ignored the comment. She walked to the kitchen and got his order so the kitchen help wouldn't have to hear him.)

Employee: *"Here you go, Mr. Morris. Thank you for your business."*

Why This Works

Amy didn't take his comments personally nor did she take the bait and become flustered. When Mr. Morris displayed pushy behavior and butted in, she politely excused herself from the phone customer and explained she'd check as soon as she was finished. Mr. Morris then played to the audience of other waiting customers, but again Amy did not show that she was bothered by his obnoxious behavior. Throughout her interaction with this customer, she stayed above the fray and, because she presented a calm and respectful demeanor she felt proud that she did not bow to his level.

Applying the Approach

When handling a customer who is obnoxious, apply the following principles to your situations:

- Remind yourself this behavior is not about you.
- Stay above the fray.
- Keep your facial expressions neutral and your demeanor relaxed.
- Speak with an interested and helpful tone of voice.
- Keep your attitude positive, no matter how much this type customer tries to bring you down.
- Ignore any name calling. Don't defend yourself. It won't do any good anyway.
- Rely on phrases of courtesy, enthusiasm, and assurance: *"Yes Ma'am, I'll be happy to check on that now."*

- If a phrase of regret is warranted or if you feel it will help: *"I apologize for that."*

- Unless the customer stops the obnoxious behavior (which isn't likely), don't try to establish a rapport; just handle the customer as expeditiously as you can.

- When you're done with the interaction, let it go. Don't talk to coworkers about it.

- Move on to your next task, feeling proud that you conducted yourself professionally and respectfully.

What to Do When the Customer Is Overly Analytical

You know this type. Just when you're sure you've answered all the customer's questions and are certain he or she is in agreement with your proposed solution, the person has one more question, often prefaced with: " But what about . . . ?" Back you go to answering yet another round of questions. People who analyze every minute detail can wear you to the ground. You want to shout: "Enough already!" But you smile and continue answering their questions because that's what you get paid to do.

Handling customers who are overly analytical can be taxing, but you can learn how to handle them by using phrases of empathy and assurance, such as *"I can sense that you're hesitant and I understand this is a big decision. I'm confident this is the best ___ based on how you said you'll be using it."* Working on establishing a rapport and finding common ground may also help overly analytical types. Often, when you paint a picture to which the customer may relate, you can get him or her on your side: *"This is the one I ended up buying for my home, and I can relate to your hesitance. I kept going back and forth between this and another model before finally deciding to go with this one."* If, however, you aren't able to move the conversation to a successful outcome, you may have to offer a stronger assurance statement: *"I've answered every question I know how to answer. I'm confident this is the best product for you but you have to make the decision."* Then offer a phrase of appreciation: *"I appreciate that you want to make sure, and I hope that you'll agree this will work for you."* Then, if the customer still does not make a decision, offer a final phrase of appreciation: *"Thank you for calling. I hope I can help you next time."*

Identifying the Behavior

An overly analytical customer may:

- Have a need for too much information.
- Want to compartmentalize general information into specific units.
- Question your judgment, knowledge, and expertise.
- Want every last detail before making a decision.
- String you along.
- Require a lot of facts before deciding.
- Be overly cautious.
- Be unable to make a decision.

Do This!

Jeff works for a company that sells home security systems. Today he's at the house of Charles Quincy, whose home was recently burglarized while he and his wife were at work. On meeting Mr. Quincy, Jeff sat down with him to assess his needs. Mr. Quincy asked many questions, and Jeff patiently answered each of them. Then Jeff made a physical assessment of the home and property and offered his recommendation. That was an hour ago and Mr. Quincy is still asking "what if" and "what about" questions. Jeff has been patient, but he realizes he's dealing with a person who is overly analytical and feels it's time to move the conversation along.

Employee: *"Mr. Quincy, I've answered all your questions to the best of my ability. Based on your needs, this is the system I recommend. Not only does it provide burglar protection, the built-in smoke detectors are also a plus."* **(courtesy, assurance)**

Overly Analytical Customer: *"What about a wireless system? Would that be better?"*

Employee: *"I understand that you want to be certain. We've already discussed the pros and cons of wired versus wireless. I under-*

stood that the wired system was what you wanted and that's also what I recommend for your home. *I'll be happy to go over those questions again, but I feel sure that this is best based on your needs."* **(empathy, enthusiasm, assurance)**

Customer: "Okay, you're right. But what if someone tries to break in through the garage? How are we protected?"

Employee: *"Mr. Quincy, having your home broken into can make anyone feel vulnerable. I'm really sorry that happened to you. I understand that you want to be sure about the security system we install, and I'm sure this is the best system for you.* We can keep going over your questions but there's nothing more I can add to what I've already explained." **(courtesy, rapport, regret, empathy, assurance)**

Customer: "I guess you're right. My wife and I felt violated and it's hard to shake that feeling. I'll go with your suggestion. How soon can it be installed?"

Why This Works

After spending so much time answering Mr. Quincy's questions, Jeff realized that he needed to move the conversation along or he'd never close the deal. He stood firm in his confident approach, offering phrases of empathy and assurance. He felt it would be helpful to offer a phrase of regret, followed by one of rapport which conveyed to Mr. Quincy that he understood the emotions people feel following a home invasion. Jeff never backed down in his resolve and, although he said it in a respectful manner, in essence he sent the message to Mr. Quincy that it was time to make a decision. Because of Jeff's confident manner, he was able to move the conversation along.

Applying the Approach

When handling a customer who is overly analytical, apply the following principles to your situations:

- Try to objectify the customer's questions. What are they really asking?

- If you suspect the customer is asking questions because of a hesitancy to make a decision, refer to the indecisive scenario to help them make a decision.

- If, however, you feel the customer is overly analytical, choose phrases of empathy and assurance to move the conversation forward: *"I understand it's a lot to think about. I'm confident that what I proposed is the best solution."*

- Establish a rapport, which can get the customer to trust you.

- Maintain a helpful attitude with these types of customers because they can easily wear you down.

- Smile and choose positive words.

- Keep a friendly facial expression and a relaxed demeanor.

- Pay attention to what the customer is actually asking.

- If you start feeling impatient or agitated, breathe deeply and slowly to calm yourself.

- Speak respectfully and confidently.

- When you feel you've spent adequate time trying to help the customer and you feel certain that you've answered the questions adequately and thoroughly, you may have to move to end the conversation: *"Ms. Customer, I've answered your questions to the best of my ability. This is the best solution I can offer you. I understand if you need more time to make a decision, and I appreciate the opportunity to help you."*

- After working on establishing a rapport, offering phrases of empathy and assurance, and feeling you can do no more, end the conversation on a positive note: *"I'll be happy to help you when you've made a decision."*

What to Do When the Customer Is Overly Friendly

You pride yourself on your professionalism when it comes to interacting with your customers. You understand the importance of establishing a rapport and you appreciate customers who are friendly because you find interacting with them enjoyable. You feel good after handling a customer whose friendliness brightened your day. But then along comes the customer who's a little too friendly, one who wants to be your friend or, worse, wants to be more than your friend. People who are overly friendly may make you feel uncomfortable, especially if the friendly gestures turn to open flirting. After all, you don't know this person who is becoming way too chummy for your comfort level.

Even if you welcome the friendliness and enjoy the flirtation, it's always best to keep your business conversations on business, so you won't send mixed messages in the event that the friendliness is a signal the customer wants more than a business relationship. Speak assertively and offer a phrase of enthusiasm, such as *"I'll be happy to help you take care of your request."* Then stick to the business conversation. If the customer continues, smile and offer a phrase of assurance: *"I'm going to take care of your request, but please, let's keep the conversation on that."* Usually, overly friendly behavior is harmless, and by reiterating that you want to keep the conversation on business, he or she is apt to comply.

Identifying the Behavior

An overly friendly customer may:

- Be chatty by nature.
- Be a touchy type of person.

- Like to flirt.
- Not understand boundaries.
- Not see the behavior as inappropriate.
- Use the friendliness as a means of getting his or her way.
- Cross the line between being friendly and making the other person uncomfortable.

Do This!

Cathy is a personal banker. She opens new accounts for customers, as well as provides any number of services that are beyond the scope of the tellers' duties. A customer sits down at her desk.

Employee: *"Good afternoon. My name is Cathy. How may I help you?"* **(welcome)**

Overly Friendly Customer: "Hi Cathy. I'm sure you can help me. I need to open a checking account."

(The customer then winked at her.)

Employee: *"I'll be happy to take care of that for you. May I have your name, please?"* **(enthusiasm, courtesy)**

Customer: "Bill Braxton. I can tell I'm in good hands."

Employee: *"Thanks, Mr. Braxton."* **(courtesy)**

Customer: "Please call me Bill. Hey, Cathy, has anyone told you how cute you are?"

Employee: *"Thank you. Now, let's get started.* Will the account be in your name only?" **(courtesy, assurance)**

Customer: "Yep. I'm single. How about you? I don't see a ring on that pretty finger. Got anyone special in your life?"

Employee: *"Well, thank you for the compliment.* But you know, my personal life just isn't exciting enough to talk about with my customers. What address should we enter for the account?" **(courtesy)**

(When Cathy replied, she smiled and spoke in a positive tone. She didn't want to offend Mr. Braxton, since she assumed his behavior was harmless, but she also didn't want to engage in a personal conversation about herself that could potentially make her uncomfortable.)

Customer: "Mine isn't too exciting either. My address is 22105 Sycamore Street. But you're really cute, even if you don't like talking about yourself."

Employee: *"I appreciate you telling me that. You brightened my day, Mr. Braxton. Now I'll explain the different types of checking accounts we offer."* **(courtesy, assurance)**

Why This Works

Even though Cathy recognized Mr. Braxton's friendliness as harmless flirting, she didn't want to encourage him in the event he mistook her friendly banter. She maintained her professionalism, politely stating that she wanted to keep the conversation on business. She didn't become offended by his comments, but rather maintained her positive attitude and spoke in a friendly tone of voice. By continuing to address him as Mr. Braxton after he said to call him Bill, Cathy sent the message that she was handling the interaction on a professional level.

Quick Tip for a Sticky Situation

If an overly friendly customer crosses the line and makes you feel uncomfortable, speak up and say so in a tactful way: *"You're making me feel uncomfortable. I'm going to take care of your request, but please, let's keep the conversation on business."* By tactfully telling the person that the behavior makes you uncomfortable, he or she is likely to stop. Use care when saying this, as you don't want to embarrass the customer, which may decrease your ability to handle the rest of the interaction successfully.

Applying the Approach

When handling a customer who is overly friendly, apply the following principles to your situations:

- Maintain a friendly, professional demeanor.
- Keep a friendly facial expression when offering a phrase of enthusiasm: *"I'll be happy to help you take care of ___."*
- Stick to the business of helping the customer, but if the overly friendly behavior continues, speak up and tactfully offer a phrase of assurance that you want to help—only with the business request: *"I'm going to help you with your request, but please, I'd prefer we stick to business."*
- When leading the conversation back to business, speak in a pleasant tone and choose nonthreatening words. Consider that the customer's behavior is harmless: *"What's the item you'd like to order?"*
- If it doesn't stop, guide the conversation back so the customer gets the hint: *"I'd rather not talk about my personal life. Now, I need to ask you a few questions in order to take care of your request."*
- Because this behavior is usually harmless, be careful not to insult or embarrass the customer. You can politely and tactfully speak up, yet maintain a friendly, helpful demeanor.

What to Do When the Customer Is Pessimistic

Generally, people can be placed in two categories: optimists and pessimists. Or . . . those who see the cup half full and those who see it half empty. You most likely already know that when you interact with a customer who has an optimistic view of life, your conversations are positive and you find it easy to communicate with this person. But what happens when you interact with customers who are pessimistic? The ones who reply to your positive comments with negative rebuttals can bring you down quickly. You've learned the importance of projecting a positive attitude, but that can be difficult when someone is continually negative. Attitudes rub off, and a negative person can pull someone down easier than a positive person can bring someone up.

You may find it difficult trying to establish a rapport with someone who continually responds with negative comments. For example, you may offer a phrase to establish a rapport, such as *"This is a gorgeous day, isn't it?"* to which the customer responds, "I saw some clouds. I think it's going to rain." You reply, *"Well, that would be good considering the drought we've been in."* The customer responds, "Not for me. I work outside and if it rains I'm at a standstill." At this point, you're beginning to recognize this customer as one who sees the cup half empty. To avoid a pessimistic person from bringing you down, it may be best to move through the steps to handle the interaction rather than continuing to offer positive comments to try to establish a rapport. Smile, maintain a positive attitude, offer phrases of enthusiasm and assurance as you handle the request, and end with a phrase of appreciation: *"Thanks for calling today. I'm glad I was able to help you."* Just don't expect the customer to respond with a positive statement. And if you are an overly cheery person, try to tone down your cheeriness with pessimistic customers. Your positive attitude is not likely to rub off on people who see the cup half empty. In fact, it may wear on them and drain that cup even more.

Identifying the Behavior

A pessimistic customer may:

- Make negative comments about everything.
- Counter a positive comment with a negative one.
- Disagree with what you say.
- Focus on the bad things that happen.
- Be difficult to establish a rapport with.
- Attempt to bring you down to his or her level.
- Try to get you to agree with negative comments.
- Be in a melancholy mood.
- Be under a great deal of stress.

Do This!

Brittany works the reservation desk for a resort hotel. She has a sunny disposition and enjoys her job, especially when she's able to help customers with their reservations. She answered a call from Mr. Hennessy.

Employee: *"Lakeview Resort, Good Morning. My name is Brittany. How may I help you?"* **(welcome)**

Pessimistic Customer: "I'd like to make a reservation."

Employee: *"I'll be happy to help you with that. How are you doing today?"* **(enthusiasm, rapport)**

Customer: "Not so good. My back is sore."

Employee: *"Oh, that's too bad. Well, then, a vacation sounds like it's just what you need."* **(empathy, rapport)**

Customer: "I don't like vacations. I'd rather be home. My wife's been bugging me to go."

(Brittany recognized that the customer seemed to be a pessimist.)

Employee: *"All right. I'll check availability right away.* May I have your name and the dates you plan to visit?" **(assurance)**

Customer: "My name is Jack Hennessy. The twenty-first through the twenty-sixth. I checked the long-range weather forecast, and it looks like it's going to rain all week, but that's the only time we can get away."

Employee: *Thanks, Mr. Hennessy. We do have availability that week, and I'll reserve a room for you now.* Would you prefer a lake view room or a mountain view?" **(courtesy, assurance)**

Customer: "If I have to pay more look at a lake, then the mountain view is good enough."

Employee: *"Yes, Sir,* lake view rooms do run a little more. I'll reserve a mountain view room for you with a check in date of October twenty-first, checking out October twenty-sixth. Does that sound all right?" **(courtesy)**

Customer: "Guess so."

Employee: *"Great.* I've made the reservation. I'll need your credit card number and you'll be all set." **(enthusiasm)**

Why This Works

As soon as Brittany realized she was dealing with a pessimist, she stopped making attempts to establish a rapport. Instead she focused on working through the steps of the interaction, speaking professionally, and toning down her usual cheeriness. She didn't take the bait by responding to Mr. Hennessy's negative comments, nor did she allow his negativity to bring her down. She maintained her positive attitude, ignored the pessimism, and worked through the interaction successfully.

Quick Tip for a Sticky Situation

If you find that a negative customer is wearing on you and the negativity is bringing you down, remind yourself that this is part of the customer's personality and has nothing to do with you. You can't control or change another person's attitude; you can only control your own. Even though it isn't likely that you're going to bring this person up, maintaining your positive attitude will stop this person from dragging you down with them.

Applying the Approach

When handling a customer who is pessimistic, apply the following principles to your situations:

- You may not realize a customer is pessimistic until you make an attempt to establish a rapport. The customer is likely to respond with a negative comment.
- Maintain your positive attitude. Don't allow a negative person to affect your disposition.
- Once you identify the customer as a pessimist, don't continue offering positive comments to establish a rapport. It's best to move through the steps of the interaction without the additional conversation.
- Don't expect that you'll be able to bring up a negative person. It's likely the person is wired this way.
- Show enthusiasm and a willingness to help. Maintain a professional demeanor.
- If you're a bubbly or overly energetic person, tone it down a notch with dealing with a pessimist. He or she is not likely to take to that sort of enthusiasm.
- At the end of the interaction, offer a phrase of appreciation: *"Thanks for coming in. I'm glad I was able to help you."*
- Resist the urge to end with *"Have a nice day."* You're apt to hear a grunt or other negative comment.

What to Do When the Customer Is Pushy

A pushy customer may be someone who has a sense of self-importance, who is rude by nature, or who feels his or her needs are more important than anyone else's. A pushy customer may also be someone, normally calm, who's in a hurry or upset and comes across in an impatient manner. Pushy people may butt in or begin a conversation with you before you're prepared.

Whenever a customer is pushy and interrupts, consider that he or she doesn't care if you're already assisting another customer. A pushy customer wants help and wants it now, but the customer you're helping should never have to wait while you help someone who has butted in. How will your current customer feel if you say, "I'll be right back," and then walk away to assist the pushy customer? This approach may satisfy the pushy customer, but the customer you've been helping is likely to become upset and you'll create another less than ideal situation you'll have to handle! Never stop in the middle of helping a customer to take care of another unless—and only unless—it's a question that can be answered quickly, in one or a few words.

Identifying the Behavior

A pushy customer may:

- Be forward, bold, impatient.
- Speak in a rushed or rude manner.
- Have a sense of self-importance.
- Butt in when you're busy helping another customer.
- Begin speaking before you're prepared to pay attention.
- Launch into the dialogue, even when it may be inappropriate.

Do This!

Sarah is a service desk employee in a party store. She's blowing up a dozen balloons for a customer who's having a birthday party for her daughter. The party begins in an hour and Sarah is working as quickly as she can when another customer approaches and butts in.

Pushy Customer: "I've looked all over the store, and I can't find anything for a luau themed party. I know you must have luau things, and I need help finding them."

Employee to first customer: *"Excuse me one second."* **(courtesy)**

Employee to pushy customer: *"Good morning. I'll be happy to help you find items for your luau,* but it's going to take me about five minutes to finish up with this customer. Otherwise, John is at the service desk, and *he'll be happy to help you now.* Would that be all right?" **(welcome, enthusiasm)**

Customer: "Oh, OK. I'll ask John. Thanks."

Employee to pushy customer: *"You're welcome. Thank you."* **(courtesy, appreciation)**

Employee to first customer: *"Thanks so much for waiting, and thanks for your patience.* Now, let me finish blowing up these balloons. *You have a party to get to!"* **(courtesy, appreciation, rapport)**

Why This Works

By first speaking to her current customer and politely excusing herself, Sarah showed that she valued the customer she was already helping. Then when she turned to the pushy customer, smiled, and spoke in a warm, courteous manner, she conveyed that she wanted to find an appropriate solution quickly and correctly. By offering to help when she finished with her current customer and also offering an alternative in the event the customer didn't want to wait, she showed that she valued the pushy customer as well. When the customer thanked her, Sarah felt good that she maintained control of the situation, handling both customers to the best of her ability. This approach made both customers feel valued. (*Note:* If the customer who butted in asked a quick question to find out if the store has items for a luau, the following response is appropriate.)

Employee to first customer: *"Excuse me a sec."* **(courtesy)**
Employee to pushy customer: *"Good morning. Yes, we do! We have tons of things for luaus in Aisle Five."* **(welcome, enthusiasm)**
Employee to first customer: *"Sorry about that."* **(regret)**

Quick Tip for a Sticky Situation

You notice that a pushy customer butts in line ahead of others who've been waiting. Is it best to ignore the situation? If you do, those customers who've already been waiting may become upset, complain to each other, take their frustration out on you, or leave their items and walk out of your place of business. Take control of the situation, smile, and say in a courteous manner: *"Excuse me, Sir,* but these other customers have been waiting ahead of you. The end of the line is behind the woman in the red top." Your other customers will appreciate you for paying attention and being assertive.

Applying this Approach

When handling a customer who is pushy, apply the following principles to your situations:

- Most likely you'll encounter a pushy customer during the Meet-and-Greet portion of your contact, so you may not have time to work on making a great first impression or building a rapport.
- Welcome this customer.
- Use phrases of courtesy, such as *"Sir"* or *"Ma'am,"* and speak respectfully.

- Display the following body language actions: Match your facial expression to the dialogue by smiling, maintaining an expression of concern, or one of interest, whichever you feel is appropriate.

- Display the following tone of voice actions: Control your voice inflection and speak in a soft, calm, matter of fact voice.

- If you weren't prepared to give your full attention, choose a phrase of regret and ask the customer to repeat the opening statement. For example, you could say: *"I'm sorry, I didn't catch what you said."*

- If the customer butted in while you were helping another, first acknowledge the customer you'd been helping.

- If you aren't able to help immediately, quickly find an alternative solution for the pushy customer and gain agreement.

- Follow up with a phrase of appreciation.

- When handling a pushy customer, work through the steps as efficiently as you can, without sacrificing effectiveness.

What to Do When the Customer Is Self-Righteous

You know the type. You probably know the person, too. That friend or family member who believes his or her point of view is the only point of view. It usually has to do with religion or politics, although it can be about any controversial subject. If you're of the same beliefs, the friend or relative has a built-in audience. If you aren't of the same beliefs, the friend or relative is likely to see you as an adversary and feel the need to convince you that you're wrong. Self-righteous people feel their beliefs are correct. They feel morally superior to everyone else. They judge others. They try to get others to agree with them. When they're your customers, they can be difficult to deal with, particularly if you do or say anything to provoke them.

When you encounter these types of customers, the best path to take is no path. In other words, don't go down the path of adding fuel to their fire. Don't respond to their statements or you're likely to engage in an argument if you disagree. And, if you agree, they're apt to continue the self-righteous ranting because they have an audience. If a self-righteous customer tries to goad you into voicing your opinion, don't go there, even if you agree. Instead, speak courteously and offer a phrase of empathy, such as *"I can tell you feel strongly about this."* If the customer continues to attempt to get you to voice your opinion, offer a phrase of enthusiasm, smile, and say, *"I'll be happy to help you with your request, but I never voice my personal opinions to my customers."* This sends a loud and clear message that you want to keep your conversation professional and focused on business.

Identifying the Behavior

A self-righteous customer may:

- Be pious.
- Be smugly convinced of his or her own beliefs.
- Want to convince others of his or her opinions.
- Be moralistic.
- Feel morally superior.
- Be judgmental toward others.
- Not want to hear someone else's point of view.
- Try to guilt others into agreeing.
- Tell others how to act.

Do This!

Michael is an architect and, during his meeting with Carl Jenkins to go over the plans for a room addition, he noticed Carl started a self-righteous rant about the government. Although Michael agrees with some of what Carl is saying, he wants to maintain a business focus rather than to engage in what he figures will be a lengthy discourse.

Employee: *"I can tell you feel very strongly about this."* **(empathy)**

Self-Righteous Customer: "I do. Don't you agree?"

Employee: *"I'm happy to review the plans to make sure we have everything the way you want,* but I'd rather keep my opinions on government to myself." **(enthusiasm)**

Customer: "Well, what's going on with the government just makes me sick. You must feel the same way."

Employee: *"Carl, how I feel doesn't matter to your room addition. Let's please review the plans, okay?"* **(courtesy)**

Why This Works

Michael held his ground when Carl tried to goad him into agreeing with his negative views on the government. When Michael didn't take the bait, Carl again tried to get him to agree. By refusing to go down that path, Michael was able to keep the conversation focused on business, eliminating a lengthy discourse. By maintaining his positive attitude and speaking assertively, Michael was able to keep the conversation on track.

Applying the Approach

When handling a customer who is self-righteous, apply the following principles to your situations:

- Don't agree or disagree with a self-righteous customer.
- Speak courteously and offer a phrase of empathy: *"I appreciate your right to your opinion."*
- Then make a business related statement by offering a phrase of enthusiasm: *"I'll be happy to help you."*
- If the customer continues, speak assertively: *"I never share my opinions with my customers. Let's get back to your request."*
- Maintain a positive, professional attitude.
- Keep a friendly facial expression and an open demeanor.
- Speak calmly and use a confident tone of voice.
- Don't start down the path by offering any comment that indicates you agree or disagree. For example: *"Hey, I don't like where we're headed as a country either, but I'd rather not go there."* You already did!

What to Do When the Customer Is Shy

Unless you're shy by nature, it may be tough to understand why people behave this way. Often, shyness is mistaken for other behaviors. You may encounter a person who you feel is a stuck up snob when, in actuality, the person is painfully shy. You may feel a person is arrogant, when the truth is that the person is not comfortable conversing with others. Because shyness can be mistaken for other behaviors, before judging and labeling a person's behavior consider that they may be shy by nature.

Interacting with a customer who's shy can be difficult. You don't know why they're acting in a certain manner, and you won't immediately recognize the behavior as shyness. Shy customers aren't likely to make eye contact, as doing so makes them feel uncomfortable. They're also unlikely to ask for help, and if you approach them with an offer to help, they may refuse it rather than enter into a conversation that's awkward to them. The best way to handle customers you suspect may be shy is to try to draw them into a conversation. Establishing a rapport is your best bet, such as *"I noticed that you were looking at that gizmo. I have one like it, and I love it. What do you think about it?"* Then proceed with your conversation by drawing the customer in: "I don't really know much about it. I was just looking at it." Offer a phrase of enthusiasm: *"If you have a moment, I'd be happy to show you how it works."* "Yeah, okay." When drawing a shy customer into a conversation, proceed with caution. Shy people also tend to be cautious, so coming across as overly enthusiastic or excited or moving too quickly into the understanding and assisting steps may cause the customer to back off. Tread lightly and you should have no trouble handling the interaction to a successful outcome.

Identifying the Behavior

A shy customer may:

- Feel apprehensive, particularly in new settings.
- Be quiet.
- Be cautious and untrusting.
- Be hesitant about interacting with others.
- Feel awkward speaking to people they don't know.
- Not make eye contact.
- Maintain a closed demeanor.
- Avoid entering into a conversation.
- Speak quietly or haltingly.

Do This!

Dani works for the local chamber of commerce as a greeter in the tourist bureau. Because the town is a historical Civil War location, the bureau has plenty of local interest brochures on hand. A woman came in, looked around, and walked over to the brochure display. Dani noticed that when she greeted her, the customer made brief eye contact and quickly looked away. Dani didn't know if the woman was snobby, disinterested, or shy, so she paid attention to her. She observed the customer seemed quite interested in some of the brochures, so she decided to see if she could draw her into a conversation.

Employee: *"Excuse me. I noticed that you're looking at the local interest brochures. Have you ever visited here before?"* **(courtesy)**

Shy Customer: "No, first time."

Employee: *"The brochure you're holding is about our art association. It happens to be one of my favorite places because some of* *the artwork depicts the Civil War battle that was fought here. I'm no artist but I do appreciate artwork."* **(rapport)**

Customer: "It looks like a nice place to visit."

Employee: *"I'd definitely recommend stopping there. I'll be happy to help you find other places you might be interested in if you'd like."* **(enthusiasm)**

Customer: "I don't want to take up your time."

Employee: *"That's what I'm here for. I'm happy to help. What types of activities do you enjoy most?"* **(enthusiasm)**

Customer: "I enjoy art. I also like to learn about local history."

Employee: *"Great. Let me pull some brochures and then I'll explain them and answer any questions you have."* **(enthusiasm)**

Customer: "Thank you. That would be very helpful."

Why This Works

Had Dani not been so attentive, this customer would likely have come and gone without any interaction. Because she took the time to draw the customer into a conversation, Dani was able to help her find places of interest. Surely, the easy manner in which Dani drew her into a conversation made the customer feel more comfortable and ultimately happy that she stopped by the tourist bureau.

Applying the Approach

When handling a customer who is shy, apply the following principles to your situations:

- Before judging the customer's behavior, pay close attention. What you may have assumed was bad behavior, such as dismissive or condescending actions, may actually be due to shyness.

- Pay attention to the customer's demeanor as he or she moves about.

- Approach the customer cautiously. Smile and keep a friendly facial expression. Maintain a relaxed demeanor when interacting with a customer who may be shy.

- Try to establish a rapport, which can help the customer relax and open up, before attempting to move through the steps to help the customer. If they're looking at a particular item, offer a comment about it: *"I noticed that you were looking at that. That's such a pretty color, isn't it? In fact, that's my favorite color."*

- The shy customer may not immediately open up and engage in a conversation, but even if he or she doesn't, you show that you're approachable and friendly.

- When you notice that the customer relaxes and is more open, try to draw them into a conversation: *"Are you looking for something in particular?"*

- Whether or not you find a way to establish a rapport, offer a phrase of enthusiasm: *"I'll be happy to help you find something if you'd like."*

- If the customer refuses your help, which may likely be the case with a shy person, continue to pay attention and offer to help when you see an opportunity.

What to Do When the Customer Is Stressed

Stress, in itself, is not a bad thing. It's how we deal with stress that can be detrimental to both our physical and emotional states and, unfortunately, in our speed-of-light paced world, no one escape stress. People have too much on their plates and often feel frazzled. Many are overworked and sleep deprived. No one, it seems, has time to kick back, relax, and enjoy. In addition, people who are affected by the negative economic climate are likely to experience an overwhelming level of stress. When stressed people are your customers, they may be difficult to deal with; they may act jumpy or seem hurried or tense. They may snap at you or argue a point without any provocation. They may also look through you, as though they're somewhere far away, not really hearing what you're saying.

When you encounter customers who are stressed, handle them by offering phrases of rapport, empathy, and assurance, such as *"It looks like you're in a hurry. I understand that feeling, and I'll take care of this right away for you."* Speaking in a soft, calming voice can help a stressed person calm down. Listen carefully to what the customer says so you don't have to ask him or her to repeat. Pay attention to nonverbal signals, both those the customer sends you and those you send the customer. Keep a neutral or concerned facial expression and smile as appropriate. Act and speak confidently and handle the customer as quickly as you're able. It may help to try to establish a rapport. For example, if a customer has a toddler tugging at her, you could say something to establish common ground: *"I've got three kids all pulling me in different directions. Some days I can't even think straight."* Then smile reassuringly and at the very least, the customer will know you understand her stress.

Identifying the Behavior

A stressed customer may:

- Be in a hurry.
- Be tense.
- Be worried.
- Be unhappy.
- Be affected by the economy.
- Take their frustration out on you.
- Speak negatively.
- Speak in short sentences.
- Act jumpy.
- Be argumentative.
- Shift their eyes back and forth quickly.
- Look through you without actually focusing or listening.

Do This!

Todd is a debt reduction counselor working for a nonprofit agency. Today he's got an appointment with Meredith, a single mom. When they spoke by phone, Meredith explained that with two young sons and an ex-husband who pays child support sporadically, she's always struggling to keep her head above water. Two months ago, the company she works for switched all employees to part time in order to keep everyone employed. Since then, Meredith has fallen behind on her bills and her credit card debt is soaring. She sounded stressed on the phone and when Todd greeted her, he could tell by looking at her face that she was stressed out.

Employee: *"Hi Meredith. It's nice to meet you in person. I understand you have a lot going on, and I'm happy to help you."* **(courtesy, welcome, enthusiasm)**

Stressed Customer: "Hi Todd. I don't have much time. My mother is watching my boys but she has to get to work."

(Todd watched Meredith carefully as she was speaking. Her lower lip quivered and her eyes welled with tears.)

Employee: *"I understand. My wife and I both work. We have three kids, and I know how tough it is trying to juggle everything."* **(empathy, rapport)**

Customer: "I just don't know what to do anymore. I hate that I'm falling behind in my bills. I don't want to end up homeless."

Employee: *"Meredith, I'm glad that you made the appointment. I'm here to help you. Together we're going to go over all your finances and come up with a plan that works for you. You're not going to end up homeless. I'm not going to let that happen."* **(courtesy, enthusiasm, assurance, rapport)**

Customer: "Thank you so much, Todd. I'm feeling better already."

Employee: *"You're more than welcome. Let's begin by looking at your income and your bills. That's probably all we'll have time for today but that's the information I need right now. Then I can get to work on setting a budget and payment plan with the creditors. Next time we meet I'll have something concrete for you to work from."* **(courtesy, assurance)**

Why This Works

In Todd's business, he's used to dealing with clients who are stressed out. But even if he didn't work for a debt reduction agency, the manner in which he spoke to Meredith would have been helpful. He paid close attention and recognized the signs of stress. He displayed empathy (without overdoing or belaboring it) and then worked to establish a rapport by finding common ground about children. By staying positive and offering phrases of assurance he confidently affirmed he was going to help her through this debt crisis. Showing his human side and that he understood helped Meredith feel comfortable and trusting toward him.

Applying the Approach

When handling a customer who is stressed, apply the following principles to your situations:

- You'll most likely notice a customer is stressed when you greet him or her.

- You'll pick up on nonverbal signals. The customer may appear to be in a hurry or tense. He or she may seem jumpy and speak in short, disjointed sentences.

- When you begin interacting with a stressed customer, offer a phrase of empathy to show you understand: *"I sense that you don't have much time."* Adding a phrase of assurance will help: *"I'm going to handle this as quickly as I can."*

- Try to establish a rapport by finding common ground: *"Every day when I leave work I have so much to do I wonder how I get it all done. Between my kids and caring for my mother it can feel overwhelming."*

- Even if the customer is not in the mood to have a conversation, he or she knows you understand stress.

- Speak softly and reassuringly.

- Handle the request as quickly as you can.

- Maintain a neutral facial expression and project a positive attitude and a willingness to help.

- Offering a phrase of empathy is the most positive thing you can do for someone who is stressed. Often, just knowing someone understands can reduce a person's stress level.

What to Do When the Customer Is Swearing

People may swear because it's a part of their vocabulary. And that's fine in certain settings, such as conversing with friends. But in a business setting, swearing is inappropriate behavior. Perhaps the customer lacks the filter that signals he or she is speaking inappropriately. Sometimes customers who are angry or upset lose control and let out a string of swear words because they're no longer thinking rationally. Whatever the reason someone swears at you, it's inappropriate behavior and you can take positive measures to stop it.

When a customer begins swearing at you, make a quick analysis of the situation before reacting. Your reaction may be to immediately say, *"I don't need to listen to this. If you don't stop swearing at me, I'll get my manager."* But try to find a more positive way to handle a swearing customer, one in which you don't have to threaten to involve your boss. If the customer is interspersing his or her conversation with swear words, they may not even realize it. Smile and use a phrase of assurance to let them know their language is inappropriate: *"I'm going to help you but I'll understand you better without the profanity."* If a customer is swearing because he or she is upset, calmly offer a phrase of empathy and assurance: *"I understand you're upset, and I'm going to help you, but I need you to stop using profanity so that I can understand what you're saying."* When you stay calm and speak assertively, the customer is likely to stop swearing.

Identifying the Behavior

A swearing customer may:

- Use this type of language as a normal part of his or her vocabulary.
- Lack the control to know when swearing is and isn't appropriate.

- Not have the filter to refrain from using profanity when speaking to different people.
- Be angry and swearing to lash out.
- Not even realize he or she is using foul language.

Do This!

Nicole is a receptionist for a realty company. Her duties include answering phones, answering questions and, most often, referring clients to the realtors who work for the company.

Employee: *"Good Morning. Kaufman Realty, this is Nicole. How may I help you?"* **(welcome)**

Swearing Customer: "Don't &$@*^@# good morning me. I left a *%&(% message yesterday for Ben, and he hasn't called me back. This is @&%*^. My time is %#*(@ valuable. Get him on the phone."

(Nicole recognized, through the profanity, that the customer was upset because he didn't receive a call back.)

Employee: *"I understand you're upset, and I'm sorry Ben didn't call you back yesterday.* He was in the field all day. He's in the field this morning but will be back in the office in about an hour. *I'll take down your information and have him call you as soon as he comes in."* **(empathy, regret, assurance)**

Customer: "I don't give a %*&#$ that he was in the field yesterday. I need to &#@!* talk to him the minute he comes in."

Employee: *Yes, Sir, I do empathize, and I apologize. I'm going to help you but I'll need you to stop swearing. May I have your name and number, please?"* **(courtesy, empathy, assurance, courtesy)**

Customer: "Sorry. I'm just really upset because it seems he's been avoiding me. My name is Scott Phillips, and my number is 212-1294."

Employee: *"Thanks, Mr. Phillips. I understand why you feel upset. I'll*

have Ben call you as soon as he comes in, and I'll make sure he calls you back before noon today. Is there anything else I can help you with?" **(courtesy, empathy, assurance, appreciation)**
Customer: "No, please make sure he calls me back."
Employee: *"Yes, Sir, I sure will."* **(courtesy, assurance)**

Why This Works

Nicole made a quick analysis and realized Mr. Phillips was upset that he hadn't been called back. By offering phrases of empathy and regret she was able to calm him down and get him to stop swearing. She also offered phrases of empathy and assurance to convey that she understood and would have Ben call him back as soon as he arrived at the office. Because Nicole paid attention and understood the reason the customer was upset, she'll follow up and make sure Ben calls him back.

Quick Tip for a Sticky Situation

If, after your first attempt, the customer continues swearing, again calmly say, *"I'm going to work with you to resolve your problem. Will you please explain what happened without using profanity?"* When you maintain a calm, yet assertive demeanor, you will help the customer calm down and realize the profanity is inappropriate and not needed.

Applying the Approach

When handling a customer who is swearing, apply the following principles to your situations:

- Pay close attention and listen carefully when a customer swears at you to determine whether swearing is a normal part of the person's vocabulary or whether he or she is upset or angry.

- Keep an open mind while listening, and don't judge the customer.

- Don't become defensive, but rather offer phrases of empathy and assurance: *"I understand that you're upset and I'm going to help you, but I'll need you to stop using profanity."*

- Stay calm.

- Maintain a passive facial expression and relaxed body language.

- Speak assertively and intersperse phrases of courtesy when conveying that you need the inappropriate behavior to stop: *"Mr. Customer, please tell me what happened without swearing."*

- Don't take the swearing personally. Usually, when customers swear at an employee, they lack the filter to refrain from using these words.

- When the customer speaks using appropriate language, show appreciation that he or she stopped swearing: *"I'm glad I was able to help you. Thanks for calling."*

What to Do When the Customer Is Threatening

Some customers, out of extreme frustration, utter threats. Most threats are harmless and meant to gain your attention or to get you to comply. People may threaten to take their business elsewhere, sue your company, or have you fired. These types of threats are ways of venting displeasure and, though the displeasure is voiced in an inappropriate manner, you recognize that the customer is angry and handle the customer to the best of your ability.

But what about a customer who threatens to harm you physically or to cause property damage to your business? These types of threats must be taken seriously. Whenever someone utters a direct threat either to you or to your place of business, you must assume the threat is real. You're no longer in a position of trying to satisfy the customer; rather, you must protect yourself. Your safety is most important. Whenever a customer utters a serious threat of the intent to inflict something harmful, such as saying, "I'm going to burn this place down" or "I'm coming over there with a baseball bat," assume the threat is real. Respond to the threat in a direct manner with a phrase of assurance: *"Mr. Upton, I'm trying to help you, but I take your threat seriously. Do you want to continue the conversation and allow me to help you?"* The customer's next statement will tell you how to proceed: "I'm sorry. I've just been so frustrated trying to get help." Again, let the customer know you take any threats seriously: *"I'm going to help you but I want you to know our company takes all threats seriously."* If, however, the customer's next statement is, "I'm sick and tired of all you people telling me you're going to help when you've done nothing: I think I need to come over there and make you help me," excuse yourself and quickly notify your manager of the threat, providing as much information about the customer as you know.

Note: This section of the book only offers suggested phrases to use to respond to threats. Your company should have procedures in place for these types of scenarios. Ask your manager for specific training on how you should handle threats.

Identifying the Behavior

A threatening customer may:

- Feel helpless and utter a threat as a means of getting your attention.
- Threaten as an act of bullying.
- Be mentally unstable.
- Be on the telephone with you and feel free to speak his or her mind.
- Be hostile by nature.
- Be physically aggressive or combative.
- Back down immediately when you confront the threat.

Do This!

Andy works for a tire store. His job duties include handling walk-in customers and answering the phone to schedule appointments. He answered the phone to hear a hostile voice on the other end of the line.

Employee: *"Good afternoon. Atlas Tires, this is Andy. How can I help you?"* **(welcome)**

Threatening Customer: "You guys sold me a bunch of crap. I've called twice already, and you just keep telling me lies. I'm sick and tired of being taken advantage of."

Employee: *"I'm sorry, Sir. I'm going to help you. May I have your name, please?* **(regret, courtesy, assurance, courtesy)**

Customer: "Yeah, yeah, you're gonna help me. Right. Just like the last two guys helped me. Upton. U-P-T-O-N. Maybe I need to come down there and crash my car through your window. Maybe that'll get your attention to help me."

Employee: *"Mr. Upton, our company takes any threat seriously. I'm going to help you but I need you to stop threatening."* **(courtesy, assurance)**

Customer: "Like I believe you? That's what the last guy said. I think your company needs to be taught a lesson on how to take your customers seriously."

Employee: *"I'm not the last guy. I'm looking at your account now, and I'm going to help you but only if you stop threatening."* **(assurance)**

Customer: "Okay, okay. I'll give you one more chance."

Why This Works

When Mr. Upton threatened, Andy immediately addressed the seriousness of being threatened. He maintained his cool, spoke courteously and calmly, and when the customer again voiced the threat, Andy told him he was going to help, but only if the threatening stopped. Andy was able to work through the interaction satisfactorily and scheduled an appointment for Mr. Upton to bring the car in. Then, after ending the call, he notified his manager, relating all the details of the conversation so that his manager could follow up.

Applying the Approach

When handling a customer who is threatening, apply the following principles to your situations:

- Ask your manager for guidelines as to how you should handle a threat. In any event, whenever you're threatened, you should notify your manager. If you feel you're in imminent danger, contact your security or law enforcement personnel.

- You may encounter a threat at any point during your interaction. The customer may utter a threat when you begin your interaction or you may notice the customer becoming increasingly agitated or angry, leading up to his or her voicing a threat.

- Customers who speak to you by phone may utter threats when they would never do so if speaking to you in person. People often feel free to speak their minds when they can't see the other person. But you should never assume this is the situation. Always address a threat.

- Whenever you are threatened, either with an indirect threat like, "Someone needs to teach you a lesson," or a direct threat such as, "I'm coming down there with a baseball bat to teach all of you a lesson," take it seriously.

- Respond to the threat by using phrases of courtesy and assurance: *"Ms. Customer, I will help you resolve this, but I can only do that if you stop threatening me."*

- Speak calmly and steadily in a self-assured, confident voice.

- If you're face-to-face with the customer, maintain a neutral facial expression and relaxed demeanor. Do not show fear.

- If the face-to-face customer doesn't back down, excuse yourself and get your manager or security personnel. Your safety is more important than trying to help someone who threatens you.

- If the phone customer doesn't back down, excuse yourself and get your manager to speak to him or her.

- To reiterate, this section only provides general guidelines for addressing customers who threaten you. Any threat must be taken seriously and your company should have specific guidelines in place. If you aren't familiar with them, ask your manager how you should handle threatening situations.

What to Do When the Customer Is Wary

Customers may be wary, particularly when interacting with certain types of businesses that have negative reputations, such as government offices. Customers may be wary about providing personal information because they feel it's going to be shared with other companies. Customers who act warily do so because they don't trust you or your business to do the right thing, they may feel uncertain about making a purchasing decision, they may feel doubtful about the information you're providing, or they may be cautious by nature and wary about everything.

Handling a customer who's wary isn't that difficult. When you demonstrate that you're ethical and honest, the customer is likely to develop trust in you and believe that you're going to do the right thing. If a customer is wary about a decision, offering a phrase of empathy, followed by a phrase of assurance may help: *"Mrs. Owens, I sense that you're being cautious about making the decision and I understand. I'm offering you the best deal I can. That's what we promise all our customers, and we take our promises seriously."* Displaying ethical behavior is important; until wary customers begin trusting you, you won't be able to interact well with them. It probably isn't going to be easy to establish a rapport with customers who are wary, but if you can get them on your side by offering phrases of empathy and assurance, you should then be able to work on establishing a rapport. *"I understand this is a big decision. I recently bought a new car and I felt the same way. When something costs that much you want to be sure you can trust the person you're dealing with."* Relating to the customer by finding common ground will help them see you as a person rather than part of the establishment.

Identifying the Behavior

A wary customer may:

- Be distrustful.
- Be uncertain.
- Be doubtful.
- Be cautious.
- Be guarded.
- Withhold key information.
- Be afraid key information will be shared.
- Say something to signal his or her wariness.
- Not make direct eye contact.
- Have arms crossed in front of body, signaling distrust.

Do This!

Annabelle is a sales associate for a car dealership. She understands that people often have negative opinions about car dealerships, so she always speaks and demonstrates ethical behavior by the words she chooses in order to establish trust with her customers.

Employee: "Hi. My name is Annabelle. How may I help you?" (welcome)
Wary Customer: "I'm looking for a new car."
Employee: "I'll be happy to help you. May I ask your name?" (enthusiasm, courtesy)
Customer: "Dave Richards."

> (Annabelle paid close attention to the customer's body language. He hadn't made eye contact, but rather shifted his gaze between the car he was looking at and the door.)

Employee: *"I know that buying a car is a big decision. Do you have a specific model in mind?"* (empathy, rapport)

> (Because Annabelle understood her customers may have preconceived negative attitudes, she empathized with Mr. Richards and immediately began establishing a rapport. She chose to ask a closed-ended question to clarify whether he had a model in mind.)

Customer: "This is the model I'm interested in. I've already done my research online, so I know the price I should pay."

Employee: *"I appreciate when my customers do that. Our dealership prides itself on offering the best prices. We guarantee that to our customers because we understand that buying a car is a huge decision."* (rapport, assurance, rapport)

Customer: "I've heard that your dealership offers that guarantee. That's why I came here first."

> (Annabelle noticed that Mr. Richards now looked at her directly and he appeared to be more relaxed.)

Employee: *"Thanks for saying that. I'll be happy to take you for a test drive."* (courtesy, enthusiasm)

Customer: "That sounds great, Annabelle."

Why This Works

Because Annabelle had a good understanding of her customers in general, she knew that she would never make a sale with a wary customer until she was able to gain the customer's trust. She did that by using phrases of empathy and assurance, choosing words that demonstrated her company's desire to treat all of its customers fairly. When she noticed that Mr. Richards was more relaxed and made eye contact with her, she knew she would be able to work through the steps of her interaction, hopefully ending with a sale.

Quick Tip for a Sticky Situation

Whenever you encounter a customer who is wary, first establish trust. Trust is necessary for you to be able to interact positively with this type of customer. Asking a closed-ended question, such as Annabelle asked Mr. Richards, will help you clarify the customer's needs because wary customers are not likely to be very communicative until they begin to trust you.

Applying the Approach

When handling a customer who is wary, apply the following principles to your situations:

- Establishing trust is the most important element in being able to successfully handle a suspicious customer.

- Conveying that you are ethical in your treatment of customers can go a long way in establishing trust with a customer who is wary, as long as you speak in a sincere manner and back up your words with your actions.

- You're likely to encounter wariness the moment you begin your interaction. Pay attention to body language, as customers who are wary may not make eye contact and their facial expressions and body language may signal distrust.

- Keep a friendly facial expression and an open, relaxed demeanor. Allow your gestures to flow naturally.

- Smile and speak in a confident tone.

- Beginning your conversation by sounding too enthusiastic may be a turn off for a wary customer. Offer phrases of empathy and assurance before moving into using phrases of enthusiasm: *"I sense that you're unsure about this and I can understand how you feel. I'm going to help you find the best product for your needs."*

- When you notice the customer begins to relax, which signals he or she is beginning to trust you, offer a phrase of enthusiasm: *"I'm happy to help you. Let's get started."*

- Pay close attention to the customer's body language to make sure he or she is building trust.

- Listen closely to the words the customer says, as that will cue you in to his or her level of trust. For example, if you've been trying to close a deal and the customer says, *"I'm not sure,"* this is a signal that the feelings of wariness may be returning. Ask more questions to uncover the customer's hesitancy.

5

Powerful Phrases
for Challenging
Employee Situations

After reading about 30 challenging customer behaviors, it's likely that you have recognized yourself as the employee in some, if not many, of these situations. You've learned how to incorporate powerful phrases and actions into your customer interactions that will enable you to successfully handle any type of difficult behavior. You should feel confident that you'll be able to regroup, recover, and handle any customer successfully.

But it isn't always the customer who behaves badly. Sometimes, it's the frontline employee who displays challenging behaviors. Sometimes, it's the frontline employee who behaves inappropriately. Have you ever been stressed out and snapped at your customer? Or dealt with a customer who pushed your buttons to the point that you blurted out something you later regretted? Or perhaps were so caught up in your work you didn't listen to your customer?

Even though you're trained to handle all customers well, at some time you're going to find yourself in a situation that causes you to perform at less than your best. And, when you perform at a level that isn't top-notch, the result is that you may display inappropriate behaviors. The bottom line is that no one is perfect and no one does everything the right way 100 percent of the time. That's what makes us human. As a frontline employee responsible for customer satisfaction, what you do when you overreact or respond in an unsuitable manner can make the difference between recovering from your misstep and ending the interaction satisfactorily or getting yourself in deeper to the point where the customer is completely dissatisfied with you or perhaps even your company.

The good news is that whether or not you've been able to recover in the past, you're going to learn how to improve your skills.... In the future, when you say or do something incorrectly, you'll be able to quickly recover by using powerful phrases and actions that turn the interaction from bad to good. You'll notice, as you read through this chapter, that phrases of regret are the common thread simply because whenever you've said or done something wrong, offering a heartfelt apology will go a long way toward mending the damage.

In this chapter, you'll learn 20 challenging situations that frontline employees may encounter. Whether or not you see yourself in any of these situations, learning how to handle yourself will enhance your interpersonal skills. Each behavior and the appropriate approach is identified with examples, along with a *Do This!* scenario containing pertinent dialogue. You'll learn how to apply each approach to your particular work environment and your customer interactions. As in the first four chapters, the powerful phrases are denoted in *italics* with the type of powerful phrase noted in **(bold)**. For some of the behaviors, a "Quick Tip for a Sticky Situation" is included as well, demonstrating how to handle a situation that can be particularly difficult.

What to Do When You Made a Poor First Impression

Customers always form a first impression. If the impression they form is less than positive, the interaction begins with a strike against you. You could be having a bad day and not keeping a pleasant expression on your face. Or, you may have overslept and aren't aware that your shirt is badly wrinkled and your hair isn't combed. Or, it could have nothing at all to do with you. Maybe, you simply remind the customer of someone he or she doesn't like, and even though you're presenting your best self, the customer forms a poor impression based on a negative bias. Whenever someone forms a poor impression of you, for whatever reason, you have to work harder to win the customer over so that you'll be able to interact successfully. Think of it as digging yourself out of a hole into which you fell.

You'll most likely know when customers haven't formed a positive impression through their facial expressions and demeanor. They may not seem too thrilled that you're the one helping them. They may not make eye contact, but rather focus on your appearance, such as the wrinkled shirt in the example above. When you pick up on cues that signal the customer has formed a poor impression of you, remember that you can change that impression through the words you choose and the actions you take. Smiling, making eye contact, and offering a sincere phrase of welcome will enhance the way you present yourself: *"Good Morning. Welcome to Kline's. My name is Zoe. How may I help you?"*

Often, offering a heartfelt greeting will change a person's negative first impression, but if you notice the customer doesn't warm to you, continue to demonstrate that you're capable, confident, and helpful. If you feel it's appropriate, offer a phrase of regret: *"I apologize for my appearance. I don't normally look like this."* Offering a phrase of regret will usually help a customer see you more positively. Following up with a phrase of rapport such as, *"My husband was late for his flight this morning, and I spent so much time helping him I was almost late myself,"* may help you find common ground with the customer. When you strive to present your best self by incorporating powerful phrases, the customer will likely see that his or her impression was not correct and you'll be able to complete your interaction successfully.

Identifying the Customer's Response

When a customer forms a poor first impression, he or she may:

- Focus more on your appearance than on what you're saying.
- Look at you in a condescending manner.
- Not make eye contact but rather look down or away.
- Not smile at you.
- Not readily accept your offer to help.
- Act in a standoffish manner.
- Demonstrate closed body language by crossing their arms in front of their body.
- Not warm up to you immediately.
- Communicate with one word or short answers.

Do This!

Zoe works for Kline's Furniture Store as a sales associate. This morning her alarm clock didn't go off and knowing she'd be late for work, she took a quick shower, put her wet hair into a pony tail, and threw on the first thing she found in her closet. On her way to work, she noticed that the blouse she was wearing didn't match her slacks. Zoe was embarrassed but she had to open the store and couldn't be late.

She got to work right at opening time and when she rushed to unlock the door, she saw a couple sitting in their car. One of the administrative assistants looked a little peeved as she waited by the door. The couple got out of their car, and Zoe noticed that they were paying close attention to her and whispering to each other. She ran and put her purse in her locker and returned to greet them. Zoe knew that in all likelihood they hadn't formed a positive impression of her. She took a deep breath before her greeting.

Employee: *"Good Morning. Welcome to Kline's Furniture Store. My name is Zoe. How may I help you this morning?"* **(welcome)**

Customer: "We just want to look around."

(Zoe saw that when the woman spoke, she didn't make eye contact but rather stared at her outfit.)

Employee: *"I'm sure I haven't presented myself very well this morning, and I apologize for that. My alarm clock didn't go off and in my rush to get dressed and out the door I didn't realize until I was almost here how I looked. I can assure you this isn't my normal style."* **(regret, rapport)**

(As she spoke, Zoe smiled warmly and made a sweeping gesture about her outfit that made the woman smile.)

Customer: "I hate when that happens. Actually, we're looking for a new bedroom suite. Can you point us in the right direction?"

Employee: *"I'll do better than that. I'll be happy to show you where the bedroom suites are located and answer any questions you have."* **(enthusiasm)**

Customer: "That'll be great. Thanks."

Why This Works

Since Zoe interacts with customers in person, she understands the importance of her appearance, so when she noticed her mismatched outfit, she realized her appearance was going to be a negative factor with customers. She knew that she would need to work harder than usual to overcome any negative first impressions. By focusing on her greeting, following up with a phrase of regret, and immediately trying to establish a rapport, she faced the problem head on and her customers responded positively.

Applying the Approach

When you made a poor first impression, apply the following principles to your situations:

- Offer a phrase of regret, such as *"I apologize if I seemed distracted when you approached me."*

- Follow up with a phrase of rapport by showing your human side: *"My only daughter just left for college, and I'm feeling sad, but that's no excuse. I should have been paying more attention to you."*

- Consider that when a customer forms a poor first impression of you, explaining yourself, as in the example above, will often get the customer on your side. Even if the customer doesn't have any children, he or she would most likely relate to and understand the employee's feelings.

- Don't belabor the point, though. Once you've explained yourself, move into the steps of helping the customer. The point of explaining yourself isn't to get customers to feel sorry for you, but to find common ground and change a negative first impression.

- If, after offering your phrases of welcome, regret, and rapport, the customer still appears to have a negative impression of you, move through the steps of helping him or her, demonstrating that you're capable of handling the request.

- If the customer forms a negative first impression based on a personal bias, you may not be able to overcome it. All you can do is handle the request to the best of your ability.

- Maintain a positive attitude, even when you sense the customer may not feel positively toward you.

- Keep a pleasant facial expression, hold your head high, smile as appropriate, maintain good posture, and act confidently.

- End your interaction with a phrase of appreciation: *"I'm happy I was able to help you today."*

What to Do When You Can't Understand Your Customer

Customers may be difficult to understand for many reasons. A customer speaking with an accent, someone with a speech impediment, or a person speaking in slang or urban lingo may be difficult to understand. In addition, if you work in a noisy environment you may have difficulty understanding someone who speaks softly or in a muffled voice. Any of these reasons will create a barrier to listening and, unless you're able to break through this barrier, you won't be able to understand and assist the customer.

You may feel embarrassed to speak up and state that you're having trouble understanding, but that's exactly what you should do. Trying to muddle through a conversation with someone you don't understand will, in all likelihood, end up frustrating both the customer and you. The best approach is to tactfully say that you're having trouble understanding. Preface your statement with a phrase of regret: *"I apologize, but I'm having trouble understanding."* Then ask the customer to repeat, using a phrase of courtesy. *"Would you mind repeating, please?"* Make eye contact and pay close attention to any nonverbal cues, which may enhance the communication message. If you're speaking by telephone, listen closely and pay attention to the customer's tone of voice. Taking extra time to listen closely and then recapping your understanding will help you correctly interpret what the customer is saying. Incorporating phrases of courtesy throughout your conversation will show that you're respectful toward the customer.

Identifying the Customer's Response

A customer who senses you don't understand may:

- Appear frustrated.
- Become embarrassed.

- Repeat the same words.
- Speak in disjointed, or short sentences.
- Speak louder.
- Walk away or hang up before completing the interaction.

Do This!

Todd is a reservation agent for an airline. He handles phone reservations, as well as customer service queries. When he answered a call using the company's standard greeting, he heard a heavy foreign accent, and didn't understand the customer's opening statement.

Employee: "I'm sorry, but I'm having trouble understanding. Would you please repeat?" **(regret, courtesy)**

Customer: "My name Mr. Lee. I need make airline ticket."

Employee: "Thank you, Mr. Lee. I understand you need an airline ticket? Is that correct?" **(courtesy)**

Customer: "Yes. Need ticket."

Employee: "I'll be happy to help you with that. What city are you flying to?" **(enthusiasm)**

Customer: "Tokyo."

Employee: "Okay, you want to fly to Tokyo. Is that correct?"

(Because of the customer's accent, Todd slowed down the conversation by asking one question at a time to enhance his ability to understand.)

Customer: "Tokyo."

Employee: "All right. You're flying to Tokyo. I can help you with that. What city are you leaving from?" **(assurance)**

Customer: "Fly Tokyo."

Employee: "Yes, Sir. Where are you now?" **(courtesy)**

Customer: "I in New York City."

Employee: "Thank you, Mr. Lee. Are you flying from New York City to Tokyo?" **(courtesy)**

Customer: "Yes, I fly."

Employee: *"Great. Thank you. I'll be happy to issue your ticket flying from New York City to Tokyo.* We have three airports in the New York City area that fly into Tokyo Narita Airport: LaGuardia, JFK, Newark." **(enthusiasm, courtesy, enthusiasm)**

Customer: "I fly LaGuardia."

Employee: *"Thank you.* You're flying from LaGuardia airport to Tokyo Narita. Is that correct?" **(courtesy)**

Customer: "Yes."

Employee: *"Great.* What is the date you want to fly?"

Why This Works

Todd knew that the customer's accent presented a barrier to effective communication, so he took extra steps to ensure he understood the customer's request exactly. He slowed down the conversation, asked one question at a time, and recapped the customer's response before moving on. When Mr. Lee didn't understand Todd's question as to where he was flying from, Todd asked the question differently. He incorporated phrases of enthusiasm and courtesy throughout his conversation to communicate that he was respectful toward Mr. Lee and that he was interested in helping him.

Quick Tip for a Sticky Situation

When you are stalled in the conversation, rather than continuing to repeat the same question, say it in a different way, as Todd did with the customer in the scenario above.

Applying the Approach

When you can't understand your customer, apply the following principles to your situation:

- Speak up and explain that you're having trouble understanding. Offer a phrase of regret, such as *"I'm sorry, I didn't understand what you said."*

- Then ask the customer to repeat, speaking respectfully and using a phrase of courtesy: *"Would you mind repeating, please?"*

- Make eye contact and pay attention to nonverbal cues that can help you understand the message.

- When asking questions, ask one at a time. Phrase your questions, using as few words as possible.

- Don't use any slang or short-cut terms a foreign customer won't understand. Use good grammar when speaking to a person from another culture.

- If you speak with a regional accent, try to speak more slowly and clearly to a person from another culture. Consider that if you're having trouble understanding, so is the other person.

- If the lack of understanding is due to a speech impediment, it might help to ask the customer to speak more slowly. Always include a phrase of courtesy: *"Will you repeat a little slower, please?"*

- Always recap your interpretation before moving on.

- Shut out external distractions, such as background noise or other conversations.

- When on the phone, look down or at your computer screen to shut out distractions. Plug your other ear if that will help. Listen to the customer's voice tone to help you understand the person's emotions.

What to Do When You Stereotype a Customer

Even though you've been trained to handle different types of customers, it's likely that you have stereotypical views about some of the people with whom you interact. A stereotype is an opinion, often negative, usually inaccurate, that we form about others who are different from us. Stereotypes are likely to be about a group of people collectively, and they're always based on personal biases. You may form stereotypes about people from another culture, teens wearing outlandish clothes and hair styles, those with multiple piercings or tattoos, or people of another color or religion. When you form a stereotype about a customer based on your personal biases about that group of people, you're likely to show, either through your facial expressions, body language, or words, how you feel. So how do you move past a stereotypical view to be able to handle each of your customers the way they deserve to be handled?

You can learn not to form stereotypes, but it will take hard work on your part to change negative biases. Basically, you'll need to train yourself to be tolerant of other people. Begin by asking, do you want others stereotyping you? Perhaps at some time it's happened; you sensed that someone was speaking or treating you as an inferior because of a stereotype the person formed about you. How did it feel? The honest answer is that it didn't feel good. You may have wondered why the person didn't take the time to get to know you rather than judge you from a previously formed negative bias. Now, think how it must feel when you speak to or treat someone else in a less than respectful manner. Don't allow yourself to think negative thoughts about someone merely because of the way a person looks, acts, or speaks. Stop judging, and give the person a chance. When it comes to your customers, that's what each of them deserves. And if you find yourself beginning to form a stereotype, take a deep breath, and stop yourself. Acting and speaking respectfully and establishing a rapport will help you break down any stereotypes you may form because it provides you the opportunity to get to know the person.

Identifying the Customer's Response

A customer sensing that you formed a stereotype may:

- Become defensive.
- Become angry.
- Leave your place of business.
- Argue with you to prove his or her worth.
- Demand to be treated well.

Do This!

Tommie is a waitress in a diner. She's outgoing and friendly with her customers, most of whom are regulars. This morning a motorcycle rider pulled up. He wore a leather jacket, had chains hanging off his belt, long hair in a ponytail, and a tattoo on one arm. She immediately tensed up and began forming a stereotype because he looked like a member of a motorcycle gang. A while back a motorcycle gang stopped at the diner and the members were rowdy, rude, and made her and the other patrons uncomfortable. She wondered why this gang member had to stop at her diner. Then she took a deep breath and reminded herself that she wasn't going to judge this man based on how he looked, but rather she would be respectful and treat him as she treated her other customers. When he entered, she smiled and greeted him.

Employee: *"Good morning. Please have a seat anywhere. My name is Tommie and I'll be right over."* **(welcome, courtesy, enthusiasm)**

Customer: "Good morning, Tommie."

Employee: *"What would you like to drink?"*

Customer: "I'd love a cup of coffee."

> (Tommie noticed that the man spoke intelligently, made eye contact with her, and smiled warmly. She began to see him differently than her stereotypical view of biker guys in leather jackets.)

Employee: *"Here you are. May I take your order?"* **(enthusiasm, courtesy)**

Customer: "I'd like the special on the board, please."

Employee: *"Great, thanks. I'll get that right out to you and hopefully it'll be before those clouds roll in. I didn't hear rain in the forecast but those clouds sure look threatening."* **(enthusiasm, courtesy, rapport)**

Customer: "Boy, I hope it doesn't. If it starts raining, I'll have to head back home. I'm a firefighter and on my days off I love to ride. It helps keep my stress level down."

Why This Works

Tommie couldn't stop herself from forming a stereotype about the man because he reminded her of the motorcycle gang that previously stopped at the diner. But she did stop herself from treating him based on that stereotype, knowing it would lessen her ability to interact well with this customer. When she noticed that he wasn't what he appeared to be, she treated the man respectfully and took the time to establish a rapport. She smiled to herself when she learned this man was a firefighter and not at all what she first thought he was.

Applying the Approach

When you find yourself forming a stereotype about a customer, apply the following principles to your situations:

- Stop.
- Remind yourself not to judge.
- Tell yourself that your stereotypes are often inaccurate opinions.
- Treat the person as you do any customer.
- Incorporate phrases of courtesy, which will help you maintain a respectful demeanor: *"Yes sir, I'll be happy to get that for you."*
- Present a positive attitude. Smile. Stay interested. Show enthusiasm. Keep an open mind.
- Keep your facial expressions positive. Make eye contact.
- Maintain a relaxed demeanor, even if you feel scared or uncomfortable at a person's appearance.
- Act with confidence.
- Establish a rapport. If you can't think of anything to say, ask: *"How are you doing today?"*
- Most importantly, look through the stereotype to really see the person you're helping.

What to Do When Interacting with a Customer Who Is Disabled

If you're not used to dealing with customers who have disabilities, you may easily become disconcerted and not know what to do or say. You may talk to the customer's companion, rather to the customer. You might stutter or stumble or offer too much assistance. You might even take over a task the customer is capable of handling. And if you focus on the disability rather than on the person, you're placing yourself at a disadvantage in the interaction.

Think how you'd like to be treated if you had a disability. You'd still be you, right? People with disabilities want to be treated like anyone else. Showing respect, using phrases of courtesy, paying close attention, and taking cues from the customer will help you determine how to proceed through your interaction. For example, if you see a person in a wheelchair struggling to reach an item, rather than getting the item, politely ask if he or she would like help: *"May I get that for you?"* Asking first gives the customer control over the decision, yet shows that you want to be helpful. If the customer accepts, smile and offer assistance; however, if the customer declines, offer a phrase of enthusiasm: *"Okay. I'll be happy to help if you need it."* Allowing the customer to stay in control while acknowledging you want to help will enable you to interact well with any customer who has a disability.

Identifying the Customer's Response

A customer who is disabled may:

- Not want to ask for help.
- Not make eye contact.
- Be reserved and not very talkative.

- Become defensive if you help without first asking.
- Feel ill at ease or embarrassed.

Do This!

Denise works for a physician as a receptionist. Although it's been a hectic morning, she's trying her best to give individualized attention to each patient. She greeted a new patient.

Employee: *"Good Morning, my name is Denise. Since this is your first visit, will you please complete this form?"* **(welcome, courtesy)**

> (Denise quickly showed the four pages of the form he'd need to fill out.)

Patient: "Yes, okay."

> (At that moment the phone rang, and Denise excused herself to answer the call. As the patient was walking away, she noticed that he clutched the clip board awkwardly and he walked with a distinct drag to his right side. She suspected that he had suffered a stroke so she paid close attention to him. He sat down and clumsily fumbled with the board, using only his left hand. She walked over, sat down beside him, and spoke quietly.)

Employee: *"I'll be happy to help you complete the form if you'd like."* **(enthusiasm)**

Patient: "Will you? I had a stroke a couple months ago, and I'm still having trouble on my right side."

Employee: *"That's too bad. I'm sure Dr. Conlan will discuss that with you. Would it be all right if I ask you the questions and then I'll write down the answers?"* **(empathy, assurance, courtesy)**

Patient: "I'd appreciate that, thanks."

Why This Works

When Denise realized the patient had a physical impairment she hadn't recognized at first, she did not act embarrassed or apologize. Rather, she sat down by the patient and quietly asked if he would like help. She gave him the control to accept or decline her assistance. Throughout her interaction, Denise was courteous, respectful, and understanding of the patient's condition. Because of the way in which she spoke and acted, she helped him maintain his dignity.

Quick Tip for a Sticky Situation

When referring to people with disabilities, putting the disability first, such as saying "the blind man," places the focus on the disability rather than on the person. Rather, focus on the person first, the disability second. For example, use terms such as, "the woman who has epilepsy," or "the person who uses a wheelchair."

Applying the Approach

When you interact with a person who has a disability, apply the following principles to your situations:

- Number one rule: Treat the person as you would any customer.
- If you don't know what to do, ask what the customer would like you to do: *"I'm happy to help you. Please tell me what I can do."*
- If the customer uses a wheelchair, make eye contact but don't hover or lean over the wheelchair. Speak directly to the customer and use your normal voice.
- If the customer has a cognitive disability, make eye contact and speak clearly in your normal voice tone. If the person has difficulty writing, offer to help: *"I'll be happy to complete the form for*

you if you'd like." Slow the pace of your conversation to allow the customer time to formulate responses.

- If the person has a visual impairment, verbalize what you're doing to help: *I'm going to calculate your total. It'll take me a moment."* Describe anything about your surroundings that may be helpful to the customer: *"There is a door about five feet ahead. I'm going to walk ahead and open it for you."*

- If a person is accompanied by a service dog, ask first if it's all right to pet the dog.

- If the person has a hearing impairment, face the person and enunciate clearly. Use simple words and short sentences.

- If the person has a speech impairment, follow the guidelines for the scenario about difficult to understand customers.

- In any situation involving an interaction with a person who has a disability, be patient and be respectful.

- If you make a blunder, don't feel embarrassed or be overly apologetic. Offer a phrase of regret and move on.

What to Do When You Make a Mistake

It's going to happen. You're human; therefore you will make mistakes. But when you make mistakes at work, it not only affects you, it may affect interactions with your customers. Perhaps your child was sick last night and you're running on empty, or you're sick and the medicine you're taking is clouding your thinking, or you're new and not fully proficient on your job, or you've got a personal problem that's been on your mind all day and you find your mind drifting when you should be listening. No matter the reason, when you're not fully with it at work, you increase the odds that you're going to make a mistake. You might input an order incorrectly, make an incorrect adjustment to someone else's account, make a promise and not follow through, just to name a few of the things that can go wrong when you're not banging on all cylinders.

It's not the fact that you made a mistake that matters; it's what you do to correct a mistake that matters. Offer a phrase of regret immediately: *"I'm so sorry I missed my commitment to call you back."* Next, own up to your mistake to demonstrate that you're accountable and then explain what happened. *"There's no excuse for what happened. I noted the memo screen on your account but failed to set a reminder for myself."* When you show that you're accountable, you may even be able to establish a rapport with the customer, who may respond: "Oh, don't worry about it. I forgot to call my mom on her birthday last month and that's a lot worse, believe me!" Now move on and offer a phrase of assurance: *"Oh my. I hope I never do that. Although I didn't call you back, I had already reviewed your account notes and I took care of the issue by. . . ."* Apologizing, taking responsibility, and confidently stating what you are going to do will go a long way in reestablishing the customer's trust in you.

Identifying the Customer's Response

When you make a mistake, the customer may:

- Lose trust in you and ask to speak to a supervisor if you don't take responsibility.
- Demand that someone else take care of the request if the customer found out you tried to cover up your mistake.
- Understand and say it's fine when you own up to your mistake .
- Thank you for making it right.

Do This!

Jason is a service rep for the local newspaper. He handles phone queries for new subscriptions, as well as customer service issues. He likes speaking to customers and enjoys his job, except that his office is understaffed and he feels he's doing the work of two people.

Employee: *"The Daily News. This is Jason. How may I help you?"* **(welcome)**

Customer: "Hi Jason. I called last month because we had a problem getting our paper. The person I spoke to said he'd adjust my next bill but I just got it and there's no credit."

Employee: *"I'm so sorry that happened. I'll take care of it right away. May I please have your account number and name?"* **(regret, assurance, courtesy)**

Customer: "Sure. It's 1113507. My name is Mrs. Thompson."

Employee: *"Thank you. May I put you on hold a moment while I check your records?"* **(courtesy)**

Customer: "Yes, that's fine."

> (Jason vaguely remembered speaking to the customer last month and when he read his computer notes, he was mortified to see that he had promised to credit her account for two week's delivery but hadn't followed through.)

Employee: *"Mrs. Thompson, thank you for waiting. I apologize for the mistake. In fact, I was the person you spoke to and, although I noted your account, I didn't follow through and make the adjustment. I try to finish my work right away, and I have no clue what happened that day."* **(courtesy, regret, rapport)**

Customer: "Jason, no need to apologize. If I had to say I'm sorry for everything I've forgotten those two words would be the most used in my vocabulary!"

Employee: *"I appreciate that you're being so kind about it. I've already credited your account for $18.84, and it will most definitely show up on your next bill."* **(appreciation, assurance)**

Customer: "Thanks for taking care of it."

Employee: *"You're more than welcome. Is there anything else I can help you with today?"* **(courtesy, appreciation)**

Customer: "No, that's it."

Employee: *"Thank you for understanding. We truly appreciate your business."*

Why This Works

Since Mrs. Thompson didn't remember whom she spoke to the previous month, Jason could have easily just let it go and issued the adjustment. The customer would have been satisfied. But what if, later that day, she remembered that he was the rep she spoke to? Even though he handled the problem, she most likely would have wondered why he didn't own up to making the mistake. Rather, he took responsibility, apologized, explained what happened, and found a way to establish a rapport. Then he assured the customer he had issued the credit and at the end of the interaction, Mrs. Thompson was completely satisfied.

Applying the Approach

When you make a mistake, apply the following principles to your situations:

- Offer a phrase of regret, such as *"I'm sorry."* It's always the right thing to do.

- Take responsibility for your mistake, and explain what happened: *"I should have input your order yesterday. I went home sick in the afternoon and it's still sitting on my desk. I know that's no excuse, and I apologize for messing up."*

- When you take the time to explain yourself, you may be able to establish a rapport with the customer. "That's okay. I hope you're feeling better."

- Offer a phrase of assurance: *"I'm going to take care of this right away. Would you mind holding a moment while I input the order?"*

- Keep a friendly facial expression and maintain a relaxed demeanor. Don't allow a mistake to fluster you.

- Speak and act with confidence. Taking responsibility for your errors shows that you care about doing a good job.

- Show enthusiasm and maintain a helpful attitude.

- End the interaction by showing appreciation for the customer's patience and understanding.

What to Do When Another Employee Makes a Mistake

It's bad enough when you make a mistake, but you've learned how to take responsibility, recover, make it right with the customer, and move on. But what about when someone else makes a mistake? Perhaps you're upset because it's yet another mistake one of your coworkers keeps making. Or, perhaps it's a new coworker who doesn't know what he or she's doing and you wish your boss would train the person already. You may feel sick and tired of always having to fix someone else's errors. You're tempted to let the customer know who caused the mistake and how it happened. You want to absolve yourself from the blame and say: *"I'm sorry about that. I see that Vanessa was supposed to call you back, and I have no clue why she didn't. I'll take care of it for you."* Saying something like this might make you feel better but you may come across as sarcastic or put upon that you have to handle the problem.

If you ever feel the temptation to blame another person, resist the urge! Customers don't care who made the mistake; they just want the problem fixed—and fixed fast. Rather than blame another employee or department for the mistake, handle the problem as if you were responsible. Offer a phrase of regret: *"I'm sorry that happened."* Explain what happened, referring to "us" or "we" rather than "that employee" or "the other department": *"I see that we were supposed to call you back to let you know when the order was shipped but for some reason, we didn't."* Next, offer a phrase of assurance: *"I'm going to contact our shipping department right now to see when the order went out. Do you mind holding a moment while I make the call?"* Then feel proud that you're able to make things right with the customer.

Identifying the Customer's Response

When someone else makes a mistake, your customer may:

- Not be happy that a mistake was made.
- Not care who made the mistake.
- Only want the problem taken care of ASAP.
- Wonder why you're blaming another person.

Do This!

Vanessa works in a women's clothing catalog ordering center. She's been assigned to handle customer service after customers place orders. She answered the following call and groaned inwardly when she saw which employee had placed the order for the customer the day before. Vanessa was tired of getting follow-up calls about mistakes this rep keeps making.

Employee: 'Good afternoon. My name is Vanessa. How may I help you?" **(welcome)**

Customer: "Hi. I placed an order yesterday, and I had asked the rep to call me back with the tracking number but I haven't heard from her. Can you check that for me?"

Employee: "I'll be happy to check on that. May I please have your order number?" **(enthusiasm, courtesy)**

Customer: "Sure. It's 91019690."

Employee: "Thank you. I apologize that we didn't call you back. I see a note on the account but for some reason we didn't call you. I'm going to check the shipping department right away and get your tracking number. Do you mind holding while I call?" **(courtesy, assurance, courtesy)**

Customer: "I don't mind at all. Thanks."

Employee: "Thank you for holding. The order was shipped yesterday and the tracking number is. . . ." **(courtesy)**

Why This Works

Even though Vanessa is tired of handling mistakes this rep continues to make, she didn't show her feelings to the customer. She remained professional, took responsibility, offered a phrase of regret, explained what happened, and then assured the customer she'd handle the request. What she does internally after this call doesn't pertain to the customer; therefore, she didn't press the issue by saying something like, "This isn't the first time this rep didn't call a customer back so I'm going to talk to her supervisor about this." The customer doesn't care and saying something like that wouldn't add anything positive to the interaction.

Quick Tip for a Sticky Situation

If, like Vanessa, you continually find yourself handling another employee's mistakes, talk to the employee first. Speak in a helpful, constructive tone: "This is the second time I've gotten a call from a customer who said you were going to call back with the order number. I saw that you noted the computer screen that you were going to call back. Here's something I do that's been a big help. In addition to noting the customer's account, I also write my commitments down on a scratch pad. That way, if I get busy I have the note on my desk." If after speaking to the employee the problem persists, you may want to refer it to your manager.

Applying the Approach

When another employee makes a mistake that you have to handle, apply the following principles to your situations:

- Never assign blame to another employee or department.
- Take responsibility for everyone in your company.
- Say "we" rather than "he," "she," or "they."
- Then follow the guidelines for times when you made a mistake by referring to the previous scenario, "What to Do When You Make a Mistake."

What to Do When You Have No Clue What to Do

It might be that you're a new employee and not fully trained, or that the customer is asking for something off the wall, or that you've never been asked this question before. You have no clue how to handle the customer's request and when that happens your confidence wanes. You don't want the customer to think you don't know what you're doing. Your job is to satisfy your customers and to find the best solution for them, so you plod on, hoping you'll get it, figure out what to do, and handle the request to the best of your ability.

Why even attempt to do that? If you don't have a clue what to do, plodding through the interaction with the hope that you'll figure it out gives you only a 50 percent chance to get it right. Those aren't the greatest odds when it comes to satisfying your customers. If you have no clue what to do, the correct approach is to say so. Don't try to cover up or act as though you know how to handle the situation. Don't guess at the solution. Your best bet is to offer a phrase of regret: *"I'm sorry. I'm not sure how to handle that."* Follow up with a phrase of assurance: *"I'm going to check with my manager to make sure I handle this correctly."* While customers appreciate an experienced employee who knows what to do, they also appreciate an honest employee who isn't afraid to admit they don't know what to do. As long as you take the time to find the best approach, your customers will always rather hear the truth.

Identifying the Customer's Response

When you have no clue what to do, your customer may:

- Not realize it immediately and continue the interaction.
- Ask for a supervisor if they suspect you don't know how to handle the circumstance.
- Want you to be truthful about the situation.

- Be unhappy if you try to cover up.
- Become upset if you guess at the answer, especially if your guess isn't correct or the best solution.

Do This!

Derek recently took a job working as a clerk in a pet supply store. In his last job at another pet shop, he prided himself on being an expert and, even though he's unfamiliar with many of this store's products, he's confident that he'll figure it all out as he goes.

Customer: "Can you help me? My cat was just diagnosed as borderline diabetic, and I'm trying to find food and treats that'll be okay for her."

Employee: "Yes, Ma'am. I'll be happy to help you. Let's go to the cat food aisle and I'll show you some products." **(courtesy, enthusiasm)**

(As Derek was walking with the customer to the cat food aisle, he hoped he'd find a brand he was familiar with. He didn't.)

Employee: "I'm sorry. I'm new here, and I was hoping I'd find a product I'm familiar with but I don't see any. I'd like to check with my supervisor rather than guess at what would be best for your cat. If you don't mind, I'll get him and be right back." **(regret, rapport, assurance)**

Customer: "I don't mind at all. I know how it feels to be new at a job, and I appreciate your honesty."

Employee: "I'm not new to the business, but I just started working at this store and the product line is a lot different than what I'm used to. I'll get my supervisor and be back soon." **(rapport, assurance)**

Customer: "Great. Thanks."

Why This Works

Even though Derek was confident that he would quickly learn the products, he didn't want to take a chance when it came to this customer's request. When he didn't find a familiar product, he did not continue trying to help the customer or fumble his way through the interaction. Rather, he immediately offered a phrase of regret, followed by a phrase of assurance that he would ask his supervisor. He also offered a phrase of rapport, and the customer related to being new on a job. Because Derek admitted he did not know how best to help the customer, she appreciated his honesty.

Applying the Approach

When you have no clue what to do, apply the following principles to your situations:

- Never try to cover up or act like you know what to do.
- Don't guess at a solution.
- When you have no clue how to handle a customer's request, say so. Offer a phrase of regret, such as, *"I apologize. I've never been asked that before, and I don't know the answer."*
- Immediately follow up with a phrase of assurance: *"I'm going to check with my manager right now and get the correct answer."*
- Look for an opportunity to establish a rapport: *"I'm glad you asked. This'll be a learning opportunity for me."*
- Maintain a positive attitude which, along with demonstrating a willingness to help, will overcome your lack of knowing what to do.
- Keep a friendly facial expression and maintain a relaxed demeanor when explaining your course of action. Doing these things will help you maintain your confidence level when explaining that you don't know how to handle a situation.
- Whenever you don't know what to do, always do the right thing and ask your supervisor to help you find the best course of action.

What to Do When You Have to Say No to Your Customer

You've heard the adage: The customer is always right. Or, the other: You should never say no to a customer. But there are going to be times when the customer isn't right. And there will be times when you're going to have to say no. Perhaps the customer asked for a product or service you don't offer. Perhaps the item is out of stock indefinitely. Perhaps the customer made an unreasonable demand. Or perhaps the customer asked you to do something unethical.

So what's the best way to say no? By learning how to say it without actually using the word. Does that even make sense? It does if you think about encounters in which you've been a customer and asked something, only to hear the response, "No, we can't do that." How did hearing the word no make you feel? It's possible that you became defensive, or frustrated, or even angry. You may even have thought, *oh yes, you will do that or I'll take my business elsewhere.* While that may be an extreme response, the truth is that no one likes being told no. So when you're on the employee end of having to say this to a customer, here's a better approach. Offer a phrase of regret: *"I'm sorry."* Follow up by explaining why you're not able to do something and focus on what you can do. *"We don't offer that service, but here's what I can do for you. . . ."* By offering an explanation and then placing the focus on what you're able to do, your customer is likely to accept your answer without becoming upset.

Identifying the Customer's Response

When you have to say no, your customer may:

- Not like hearing the word no.
- Become defensive, upset, or angry.

- Demand that you comply with the request.
- Try to goad you into saying yes.
- Continue asking with the hope of wearing you down.

Do This!

Kelly works for a health insurance company. Her primary responsibility is to handle customer service requests over the telephone.

Employee: *"American Health Insurance. This is Kelly. How may I help you?"* **(welcome)**

Customer: "Hi. My name is Sandra Daniels. I'm calling to check on a claim for my mother."

Employee: *"I'll be happy to help you, Ms. Daniels. May I have your mother's social security number, please?"* **(enthusiasm, courtesy)**

Customer: "Sure. It's 554. . . ."

Employee: *"Thank you. It'll take me just a moment to pull up the account information. How are you doing today?"* **(courtesy, rapport)**

Customer: "I'm doing great, thanks."

Employee: *"Ms. Daniels, I have the account information, but I'm sorry, I don't see your name on the account as someone I can speak to about it. Due to our privacy policy, I can only speak to your mother. I'll be happy to speak with her if she's available."* **(courtesy, regret, enthusiasm)**

Customer: "Oh, I was afraid of that. We just moved her into assisted living. She has Alzheimer's and wouldn't be able to understand you. I'm going to be handling her accounts, and I'm just trying to check on the latest claim her doctor submitted. Look, I'm her daughter, and I've been going through so much trying to get her moved, can't you check it for me this once?"

Employee: *"I understand, and I'm sorry for what you're going through. We do have a privacy policy, which I'm sure you can appreciate. Unless we have written documentation, I'm not able to give out any information to anyone but your mother. Let's find a workable solution so that I can add you to her account. Do* *you have a power of attorney agreement?"* **(empathy, regret, assurance)**

Customer: "Yes, I just signed one last week."

Employee: *"Good. If you'll draft a short letter explaining the situation, include your social security number, sign the letter, and fax it to me along with the power of attorney agreement, I'll add your information to the account and then I'll be able to discuss it with you."* **(enthusiasm, assurance)**

Customer: "Okay. It'll add to my already long list of things to take care of, but if I have to I have to."

Employee: *"Thank you for understanding. I'm not trying to make it difficult for you, but we do have to protect the privacy of our clients. I'll give you my fax number and as soon as I receive the paperwork from you I'll add it to her account and call you back."* **(appreciation)**

Why This Works

Kelly's company had a strict policy regarding the privacy of its clients. When Kelly checked the records and didn't see Ms. Daniels' name on the account, she knew she'd have to refuse help. However, she was able to decline without saying the "no" word and offered an explanation as to why she wasn't able to comply with the request. Then she explained what she could do to help the woman. Even though Ms. Daniels tried to goad her into complying this one time, Kelly held her ground, maintained a positive attitude, and focused on what she could do to help.

Quick Tip for a Sticky Situation

If a customer asks for a product that your company doesn't provide and you know of another company that does, why not offer that as an alternative solution? Think of how good your customer will feel if you say: *"I'm sorry, we don't offer that, but I know Jenson's Hardware does."* Your customer is likely to be pleasantly surprised that you're offering up information about your competitor and will leave your place of business with a positive feeling about you and your company.

Applying the Approach

When you have to say no, apply the following principles to your situations:

- Don't lose your confidence or fumble your words.

- Offer a phrase of regret, such as, *"I'm sorry. I'm not able to order that."*

- Follow up with an explanation: "That product is on backorder indefinitely."

- Then offer a phrase of enthusiasm indicating what you can do: *"We have a replacement that's actually an upgrade. It's very similar, and it's in stock. I'll be happy to order that for you at no extra cost."*

- Offer a phrase of empathy to show the customer that you understand the imposition: *"I understand that you had your heart set on that, and I wish we had it available for you."*

- Maintain your positive attitude by focusing on what you can do rather than on what you can't do.

- Keep a friendly facial expression and act with confidence.

- If a customer tries to get you to do something unethical, always act with integrity and do the right thing.

What to Do When You've Said Something Tactless

If you've never been guilty of saying something tactless, then congratulations! But the vast majority of us have inadvertently said something we shouldn't have said. And, most likely it's happened more than once. Often, the second the words flew out of your mouth, you realized and regretted saying them. You may have said something that was insulting or demeaning or hurtful. It's bad enough when you say something tactless to a friend or family member, but when it comes to customers who don't know you, it can be devastating to your present and future business relationship.

Words are like arrows. Once shot out of your mouth, they can't be taken back. They're aimed at a target, and they usually hit the mark. When you blurt out something tactless, you can't take back the words, but you can offer an apology. The first words out of your mouth should be: *"I'm so sorry I said that."* It may be best to leave it at that and move on, but if you feel an explanation is appropriate, offer one: *"That type of talk isn't meant for our customers to hear, and I shouldn't have said it. In fact, it's never appropriate."* Follow up with a phrase of assurance: *"I'm going to take care of your request right now."* Phrases of empathy or rapport may be used if you feel they'll help: *"I understand that I may have upset you,"* or *"I know better than to talk like that."* Maintain a positive attitude and a friendly facial expression and try to get the customer on your side by handling the rest of the interaction professionally.

Identifying the Customer's Response

When you said something tactless, your customer may:

- Look peeved.
- Display closed body language.

- Lose trust in you.
- Become upset or angry.
- Become noncommunicative.
- Consider going to another place of business.

Do This!

Ashley is a sales associate for a bridal shop. In addition to carrying bridal wear, the shop sells mother-of-the-bride dresses, evening gowns, prom dresses, and other party clothes. A rather large woman walked into the shop and Ashley offered her standard greeting.

Employee: *"Hello. My name is Ashley. How may I help you?"* **(welcome)**

Customer: "Good morning. I'm on the symphony fundraiser committee, and I'm looking for an evening gown for the gala event. Do you carry size twenty?"

Employee: *"Yes, we sure do! I'll be happy to help you find something. Let's walk over to our wide load department."* **(enthusiasm)**

> (As soon as Ashley said "wide load" she was mortified by her blunder. That was an inside joke she and her co-workers used to describe the large size department.)

Employee: *"Oh my. I'm so sorry I used that term."*

> (The customer glared at her.)

Employee: *"I realize that what I said was completely inappropriate. I know better, and I understand that you're probably upset."* **(rapport, empathy)**

Customer: "Well, I know I'm a large woman, but I've never heard the women's department called wide load before."

Employee: *"Again, I apologize. Words can be very hurtful, and I've learned a valuable lesson from what I've said. Going forward, I'm going to remember how hurtful those words were. I can assure* *you that what I said was in no way directed at you personally."* **(regret, rapport)**

Customer: "Well, you're not the first person to comment on my weight. I've been heavy all my life. It's been such a struggle trying to lose weight but I keep trying."

Employee: *"I understand. Let's walk to the women's department. We have many styles that are very flattering, and I'm sure I can help you find something that'll look stunning on you."* **(empathy, assurance, rapport)**

Customer: "If you can do that, I'll shop here all the time!"

Why This Works

As soon as the words flew out of Ashley's mouth, she regretted saying them. She immediately offered a phrase of regret and, when she saw that the customer was put off by her comment and glared at her, she followed up with a phrase of empathy. There was no way to justify what she had said, so she tried to gain the woman's trust by attempting to establish a rapport. Because she was sincere in her apology and phrases of empathy and rapport, she was able to get the customer on her side. They established a rapport about the woman's weight struggles and Ashley was able to continue the interaction on a positive note.

Applying the Approach

When you said something tactless, apply the following principles to your situations:

- Immediately offer a phrase of regret, such as, *"I feel terrible that I said that."*
- Offer an explanation if you feel it will help: *"In fact, I know better than to ever say something like that."*

- A phrase of empathy can often help: *"I'm sure I upset you, and I'd be upset too if someone said that to me."*

- So can a phrase of rapport: *"I learned a valuable lesson about thinking before I open my mouth."*

- Work on establishing trust by saying a phrase of assurance: *"I'm going to take care of this for you right now."*

- Maintain a caring facial expression and make eye contact.

- Demonstrate your positive attitude by moving on and helping the customer.

- Choose positive words throughout the rest of the interaction.

- Say something in your phrase of appreciation to show the customer you are truly sorry for what you said: *"Thank you so much for allowing me to help you."*

What to Do When You've Talked Over Your Customer's Head

You're experienced. You know your products and services inside and out. You know what's best for each of your customers and speak with confidence when explaining your reasons and offering your solutions. But . . . you're so experienced you have trouble speaking at a level your customers understand. You may use company lingo or acronyms when describing your products. You may use overly complex terms or forget that your customers don't possess the level of knowledge you do. When you're met with a blank stare, you realize that you're talking over your customer's head.

When you recognize this, you're going to have to back up a step (or two or three), quickly analyze your customer's level of knowledge, and speak in a manner the customer can understand. Offer a phrase of empathy: *"I can see why you're looking at me like that."* Offer a phrase of regret if necessary: *"I apologize that I've been talking in overly technical terms. I'll start over and explain this product in a manner that's easier to understand."* Now ratchet it back a notch and speak to your customer's level of understanding.

Identifying the Customer's Response

When you speak over your customer's head, he or she customer may:

- Be embarrassed.
- Feel dumb.
- Stare at you blankly.
- Speak up and ask you to repeat what you've said.
- Speak up and ask you to say it in easier to understand terms.

Do This!

Fred is a sales associate in a home improvement store. He was a general contractor and, after turning over his business to his sons, he felt he was too young to retire so he took this job. Working for a home improvement store is a good fit for his level of expertise. He enjoys speaking to customers and helping them with their projects. Often, though, he finds himself speaking in overly technical terms that his customers don't understand.

Customer: "Can you help me? I want to screen in my patio. I took all the measurements and drew this diagram to show what I want to do. I just need help getting the right materials."

Employee: *"I'll be more than happy to help you with that. Enclosing a patio shouldn't be difficult at all for you. I like vinyl spline screening best because it's easy to install. Let's go to that department, and we'll get you set up. You'll need the base attachment track, vinyl splines, and the screening. . . ."* **(enthusiasm, rapport)**

(Fred noticed the customer looked confused. Although the man hadn't interrupted him, Fred realized the man had no clue what he was talking about.)

Employee: *"You know, I just realized that I launched into explaining vinyl spline screening without first explaining what that is. You may have no idea what I've been talking about."* **(empathy)**

Customer: "This is all new to me. I've never done anything like this before, and it's a project I'd like to try it."

Employee: *"I'll be happy to fully explain vinyl spline screening so you understand exactly what to do. Then we'll get you set up. It's really a very simple system. . . ."* **(enthusiasm)**

Why This Works

Fred is very knowledgeable about home improvement, and one of the things he likes best about his job is helping his customers find the best solution for their needs. Because he knows so much about the subject, though, he often uses terms that are unfamiliar to his customers. He quickly realized that this customer didn't understand what he was saying, so he offered a phrase of empathy and then started over.

Quick Tip for a Sticky Situation

If you have trouble speaking in basic terms, remind yourself that you weren't always so knowledgeable. Remember how you felt when you were learning your company's products and services. This should help you find ways to speak so that your customers understand what you're saying to them.

Applying the Approach

When you speak over your customer's head, apply the following principles to your situations:

- When you pay close attention to your customers, you're going to know that you're speaking in terms they don't understand.
- You'll notice a change in their facial expression: a blank stare, a confused look, or they may look down rather than at you.
- They may also look embarrassed.
- Offer a phrase of empathy, such as *"I realize I've been speaking in overly complicated terms, and you may not have understood any of it."*

- Quickly assess where you lost your customer, go back and repeat, choosing different words: *"Let me back up. This product is designed. . . ."*

- Smile and show your enthusiasm when offering your explanation: *"Let's try it out. I'll be happy to show you how it works and you can try it for yourself."*

- Feel good that you're able to redirect the conversation and help your customer understand what you're saying to them.

What to Do When You've Patronized a Customer

To patronize someone means to speak or act in a manner that comes across as superior in nature. You may inadvertently handle a customer in this manner. For example, you may speak to an elderly customer as though he or she were a child. You may speak excessively loudly or slowly to a customer with a hearing disability. You may refer to a member of the other sex by an inappropriate label, such as "Honey" or "Sweetie." If you're interacting with a customer who uses a wheelchair, you may speak to the person's companion. You may not even realize you're doing these things and that's why this topic is being addressed.

Think about recent customer contacts you've had with customers who were elderly, or had a disability, or were of the opposite sex. Now think how you spoke to them. Honestly analyze your behavior to see if you've been guilty of speaking in a patronizing manner. If the answer is yes, then knowing that you've done this in the past will make you aware not to do it in the future. If you ever find yourself in a situation in which you're patronizing a customer, stop, back up a step, and regroup. If the customer doesn't seem bothered by your actions, there's no need to address how you spoke. Stop the patronizing behavior and complete the interaction. If, though, you think the customer was angered or upset, offer a phrase of regret: *"I'm so sorry I spoke to you like that."* If you feel it'll help, offer a phrase of empathy: *"I wouldn't like it if someone spoke to me the way I just spoke to you."* Then move on and complete the interaction, treating the customer with respect.

Identifying the Customer's Response

When you've patronized a customer, he or she may:

- Not say anything.
- Think that you feel you're superior.

- Feel dumb.
- Feel offended.
- Lose self-confidence.
- Become frustrated.
- Think you're rude.

Do This!

Mary is a cashier in a grocery store. Productivity is important in her job, and she prides herself on being able to scan items quickly while casually conversing with customers. An elderly woman is having trouble putting her items on the counter, which is slowing Mary down.

Employee: "Sweetie, can you get those cans on the counter for me, please? There's still some in your cart. You can do it." **(courtesy)**

Customer: "I'm going as fast as I can."

Employee: "Oh I know you are, Sweetie. Would you like me to help you?"

Customer: "No, I'm perfectly capable."

> (With that comment, Mary realized she had patronized this customer, who was likely feeling offended by her manner of speaking. She had treated the customer as though she was a three-year old and regretted doing so. Because the customer appeared to be offended, Mary felt an apology was in order.)

Employee: "I'm so sorry I spoke to you like that. I have a young grandchild I spend a lot of time with and sometimes when I'm at work I forget that I'm not speaking to her." **(regret, rapport)**

Customer: "That's all right."

Employee: "Well, it really isn't all right. I'd be upset if someone spoke to me like I spoke to you. Thanks for being so understanding." **(empathy, courtesy)**

Why This Works

Mary quickly realized that she had patronized this elderly customer. Because she was paying attention she noticed, through the customer's body language and facial expression, that the woman appeared to be offended. Mary regretted the manner in which she had spoken and took steps to rectify the situation by offering a phrase of regret. Mary then was able to turn the conversation around and remind herself not to treat her customers like that in the future.

Applying the Approach

When you've patronized a customer, apply the following principles to your situations:

- If the customer doesn't appear to be bothered, then move on and handle the rest of the interaction to the best of your ability.
- You may realize, by paying attention to your customer's facial expression and body language, that you said or did something that was patronizing.
- If the person appears upset, offended, or angry offer a phrase of apology, such as *"I apologize for my actions."*
- Also, offer a phrase of empathy to show the customer you're truly sorry: *"I understand how I must have made you feel."*
- Speak in a respectful tone and keep a pleasant facial expression.
- Look for an opportunity to establish a rapport with the customer.

What to Do When You Didn't Listen to Your Customer

The importance of listening is stressed throughout this book. As an employee responsible for customer service, you understand how crucial listening is. You know that if you don't listen, you're going to have to ask your customer to repeat what he or she has said. You know that if you don't listen, it's going to take longer to understand your customer's request. And you know that if you don't listen, you may make an incorrect decision for your customer. But you're also human; therefore, there are going to be times when you aren't going to listen to your customer as carefully as you should. You may be distracted by external noise, pay more attention to someone else's conversation, be caught up in your thoughts, or not be feeling well. There are many reasons that keep you from listening, even though it's your job to listen.

When you realize that you haven't listened to your customer, you may decide to continue the conversation, hoping that you'll pick up where you drifted off. Why take that chance? Your customers will appreciate it more if you pause in the conversation and own up to your misstep. Offer a phrase of regret: *"I'm so sorry. I didn't hear what you said about the problem you're having."* Explain if that will help: *"It's very noisy here, and I'm having trouble filtering out the noise."* Then pay close attention and make sure you don't have to ask the customer again to repeat. If face to face, make eye contact and keep your focus on your customer. If on the phone, interject comments to show you're listening, such as "I see" or "hmm."

Identifying the Customer's Response

When you didn't listen, your customer may:

- Wonder if you're interested in helping.
- Not appreciate having to repeat.

- Feel you're not going to handle the request correctly.
- Wish someone else was taking care of their request.

Do This!

David works in a sporting goods catalog call center, handling customer service calls after orders are placed. While he was doing busy work as he waited for the next call to come in, he overheard his coworker having a comical conversation with a customer who must have been intoxicated. David stood up and began making funny faces and mouthing exaggerated expressions to the coworker. Because he was paying more attention to his coworker's conversation, when his next call came in, he didn't hear the customer's opening statement.

Customer: "Hello, are you there?"

Employee: *"Yes Ma'am. I apologize. It's very noisy here, and I wasn't able to hear you. My name is David. How may I help you?"* **(courtesy, regret, welcome)**

> (David heard the woman sigh loudly, and he realized that he'd have to pay very close attention and completely shut out his coworker's conversation. He plugged his other ear and looked down at his desk to block any external distractions.)

Customer: "I'm trying to find out when my order will be shipped."

Employee: *"I'll be happy to check on that for you. May I please have your name and the order number?"* **(enthusiasm, courtesy)**

Customer: "Joan Everett. The order number is 9847002."

Employee: *"Thank you, Ms. Everett. I'm checking that right now for you. How are you doing today?"* **(courtesy, assurance, rapport)**

Customer: "I'm doing okay. Boy, you're right about the noise there. I can hear it too."

Employee: *"It can get a little loud, but I should have been able to shut out the noise when you came on the line. I've got your or-*

*der on my screen, and I'm happy to tell you it was shipped to-
day."* **(rapport, enthusiasm)**
Customer: "Excellent, thank you."
Employee: *"May I help you with anything else?"* **(appreciation)**
Customer: "No thanks."
Employee: *"Thank you for your business."* **(appreciation)**

Why This Works

David hadn't been paying attention but as soon as heard his customer
he realized that he'd have to ask her to repeat and she wasn't going to
be thrilled about having to do so. He immediately offered an apology
and an explanation and then paid complete attention, hoping to overcome the poor first impression he had made. At first peeved, Ms. Everett calmed down after hearing his explanation. David was even able
to establish a rapport because he had demonstrated that he regretted
not hearing and then paid close attention.

Applying the Approach

When you didn't listen to your customer, apply the following principles to your situations:

- Offer a phrase of regret, such as *"I apologize."*

- Offer an explanation if appropriate: *"My headset wasn't on properly."*

- If in person, demonstrate through your facial expressions and
  body language that you're paying close attention.

- Shut out all distractions.

- If in person, keep your focus on the customer and maintain eye
  contact.

- If on the phone, look down or at your computer screen. Plug your
  other ear if that will help you hear.

What to Do When You Annoy Your Customer

You may be asking for too much information or for information that's too personal. You may be coming across as though you're interrogating the customer. Or perhaps you have a lengthy computer process to complete. Whatever the case, your customer's starting to look annoyed. You pick up on the change in mood but you have to get through the contact, even if it means asking more questions or requiring more personal information or taking more time.

Whenever you pick up on clues that signal a change in your customer's mood, stop and figure out what you're doing. Once you work out the reason for the shift in the customer's mood, offer a phrase of regret: *"I'm sorry if it seems I'm asking too many questions"* or *"I apologize that I need all this personal information."* Then follow with a phrase of empathy and an explanation: *"I'd feel the same way if I had to answer all these questions, but I need this information in order to process your request."* Usually, when you apologize, empathize, and explain, your customer will calm down and comply.

Identifying the Customer's Response

When you're annoying your customer, he or she may:

- Wonder why you need all the information.
- Wonder what's taking you so long.
- Become agitated.
- Show his or her displeasure by saying something negative.
- Refuse to provide any more information.
- Ask to speak to a supervisor.

Do This!

Kurt is an accountant in a small firm. He's working with a new client who is a small business owner. He has to ask a lot of questions to complete his new client assessment form and the client is becoming annoyed. Kurt figures it's because he's asking too many questions, some of which may not seem pertinent to accounting.

Client: "I have one son who's fourteen."

> (When the man answered this question, he sighed loudly.)

Employee: *"I apologize for asking so many questions. I can understand that you're wondering why we need all this personal information. We like to have a complete profile on our clients, which often gives us clues that can lead to tax breaks."* **(regret, empathy)**

Client: "Well, it seems a little excessive."

Employee: *"Yes, sir, it would to me too if I didn't work here. I can assure you the reason for the information is to find all the tax breaks we can for you."* **(courtesy, empathy, assurance)**

Client: "All right. If you can find tax breaks it'll be worth answering all these questions."

Employee: *"That's our goal. And the good news is that we're almost finished."* **(enthusiasm)**

Why This Works

As soon as Kurt noticed that the client was becoming annoyed he figured it was due to the number of questions he was asking. He offered a phrase of regret, a phrase of empathy, and most importantly, he explained why he was asking the questions. He followed up after the client made the comment that the questions seemed excessive by empathizing and explaining to the client the purpose for the information.

Quick Tip for a Sticky Situation

Kurt could have avoided this conversation all together had he explained what he was doing prior to asking the questions. Before launching into a long list of questions, which may seem like an interrogation, saying something like, "I'm going to need to ask you a list of questions to complete our questionnaire. The reason we ask these questions is to make sure we find all the tax breaks we can," will help the customer know what's coming. But since Kurt didn't do that, he handled the situation well as soon as he noticed the client was becoming annoyed.

Applying the Approach

When you're annoying your customer, apply the following principles to your situations:

- Offer a phrase of regret as soon as you notice your customer is becoming agitated or upset: *"I apologize it seems to be taking me forever."*
- Follow with a phrase of empathy and an explanation, such as *"I understand that this process may seem slow to you but I'm required by law to compile all this information."*
- Get the customer on your side before proceeding. It can help to offer a phrase to establish a rapport: *"As slow as it may seem to you, imagine how slow it seems to me. I do this all day!"*
- Maintain your positive attitude and you should be able to get the customer on your side so that you can proceed.
- Speak respectfully when asking the questions.

What to Do When You Say Something Sarcastic to Your Customer

Now that we've covered a situation in which you've annoyed your customer, what can you do when it's your customer who's annoying you? What can you do when you let your annoyance grow and say something sarcastic? The customer may be demanding, condescending, or demeaning. You're trying to hold it together, but then you hear yourself saying: "Sir, I'm doing the best I can." And you said it sarcastically, putting the most sarcastic emphasis on the word "sir." As soon as you said the words you realized how you sounded and you know it's not how your company expects you to speak to your customers.

When you've said something sarcastic, immediately offer a phrase of regret, even if you feel your sarcasm was warranted: *"I'm so sorry for my tone."* Now, calm yourself, and remind yourself not to take the customer's treatment of you personally. Gather your inner strength, suck it up, and move on. Take the high road and maintain a positive attitude. Pay attention to your tone of voice to make sure you sound respectful and helpful. If the customer doesn't readily accept your apology, offer a phrase of empathy: *"I understand why I upset you and again, I apologize."* Make eye contact when you say this, hold your head high, and act with confidence. As you continue through the steps to help the customer, and speak respectfully, you'll be able to end the interaction on a positive note.

Identifying the Customer's Response

When you say something sarcastic, your customer may:

- Stare at you open mouthed.
- Become upset, angry, or belligerent.

- Demand to speak to your supervisor.
- Not readily accept your apology.
- Feel you're not the best person to handle the request.
- Take a while to warm up to you.

Do This!

Thomas is a computer tech. He's at the home of Mr. Wilson, whose hard drive crashed. Thomas has been working on the computer problem for over an hour. During that time, Mr. Wilson has hovered over him and has continued to harp about the amount of time the work is taking. Thomas has held it together but he's getting tired of the man breathing down his neck and making comments.

Customer: "How much longer is this going to take? I'm paying you by the hour, and you're just sitting here doing nothing. I don't like to be taken advantage of."

Employee: "Sir, I'm working as quickly as I can. It's a little unnerving trying to work with you hanging over my shoulder."

> (Oops! Thomas said that sarcastically, and even though he knew he shouldn't speak like that, he'd had it and couldn't help himself. But as soon as he said what he said, he realized he'd crossed the line.)

Employee: "Mr. Wilson, I'm so sorry I said that." **(courtesy, regret)**

Customer: "Well, I don't like your tone."

Employee: "I understand if you're upset by what I said and, again, I apologize. It may seem as though it shouldn't take this long, but I'm working as quickly as I can. Right now I'm running a diagnostic and there's not much I can do until that's complete. Then I'll be able to pinpoint the trouble and get you up and running." **(empathy, assurance)**

Customer: "Oh, okay. Any idea how long that'll take?"

Employee: "It's about seventy-five percent complete, so about another fifteen minutes. *Believe me, if I could speed up the process I'd be happy to do so. I don't like this part of the trouble shooting because there's nothing I can do until it's complete other than to monitor the results.* " **(enthusiasm, rapport)**

Customer: "Well, I wouldn't even know where to begin."

Employee: *"That's what I'm here for. This is what I went to school for and I really enjoy my work. I know how frustrating it can be when your computer crashes. I've been doing this work for seven years, and I'm confident I'll get your computer fixed soon. I've already seen one item that could be the cause of the problem."* **(rapport)**

Why This Works

As soon as Thomas uttered his sarcastic comment, he didn't wait to gauge Mr. Wilson's response, but immediately offered an apology. He knew that no matter how a customer spoke to him, he knew better than to become sarcastic. But it happened and he regretted it. When Mr. Wilson didn't readily accept the apology, Thomas offered a phrase of empathy and then worked hard to establish a rapport by explaining what he was doing. Eventually, he and Mr. Wilson found common ground and as he waited for the diagnostic to finish running, he used the time to tell Mr. Wilson about his background.

Applying the Approach

When you make a sarcastic comment, apply the following principles to your situations:

- Something happened to cause you to become sarcastic, so quickly calm yourself down.

- If it was the manner in which the customer treated you, remind yourself not to take it personally.
- Focus instead on the proper way to speak to the customer.
- Focus on presenting a positive attitude.
- Offer a phrase of regret: *"I'm so sorry I said that to you."*
- If the customer doesn't accept, offer a phrase of empathy: *"I understand your feelings, and again, I'm sorry. I was wrong to speak to you like that."*
- Then speak courteously and respectfully.
- Try to establish a rapport with the customer to get the customer on your side.

What to Do When You or Your Customer Is Embarrassed

Embarrassing moments happen to everyone. Someone may do something that makes you feel embarrassed. You may do something that embarrasses someone else. Or you may do something to embarrass yourself. It's how you recover from these moments that can further your feelings of embarrassment or allow you to get past the moment and move on. When interacting with customers, your words can ease the situation and enable you to complete the interaction successfully.

You never know when someone is going to feel embarrassed. People have different comfort levels and something that embarrasses one person may not even faze another. Embarrassment often arises out of feelings of insecurity or a lack of confidence. Offering a phrase of empathy can help: *"I can relate to how you feel but really, there's no reason to feel embarrassed."* Trying to establish a rapport can also be useful when a customer feels embarrassed: *"I can't tell you how many times I've done that. I've learned not to take my mistakes so seriously or I'd have a red face all the time!"* Humor can diffuse an embarrassing situation when used in a phrase of rapport: *"Just last week I had to give a presentation to upper management and when I got up to speak I noticed a coffee stain on my shirt. Now that was embarrassing!"* Helping the customer feel comfortable by showing your human side and maintaining a relaxed, friendly demeanor will lessen the embarrassment.

Identifying the Customer's Response

When someone is embarrassed, he or she may:

- Avoid eye contact.
- Become flustered.

- Get red in the face.
- Not know what to say.
- Say something self-deprecating.
- Avoid a conversation with you.

Do This!

Sam is a salesperson for a car dealership. He just sold a new vehicle and was printing out the paperwork when the customer, Ms. Stevenson, spilled coffee all over the contract. She was so embarrassed she turned bright red and started blotting up the coffee with tissue. Sam wasn't surprised because this customer had been jumpy and edgy from the beginning. Now he'd have to start the process all over. Then Sam realized the customer was embarrassed and he needed to say something to lessen her feelings of embarrassment if he wanted to complete the sale on a positive note.

Customer: "I can't believe I did that! Now you're going to have to start over. I'm so sorry."

Employee: *"Don't even worry about it, Ms. Stevenson. It's all right."* **(courtesy)**

Customer: "No, it isn't all right. I feel so dumb."

Employee: *"Hey, don't feel that way. If I felt that way about everything I've spilled, I'd never feel smart. It was an accident. We'll get it cleaned up and I'll print the contract again."* **(empathy, rapport)**

> (With that comment, she smiled and Sam was pleased that he had diffused the situation and lessened the customer's embarrassment.)

Customer: "Thanks, Sam. I guess I didn't need that coffee anyway. This is my first time buying a car and I'm nervous enough without it."

Why This Works

As soon as Sam realized the customer was embarrassed, he knew he needed to quickly say something to lessen her feelings. He was courteous, respectful, and empathetic. When he internalized feeling embarrassed, he helped the customer save face and they were able to move on and complete the sale.

Quick Tip for a Sticky Situation

If you did something to embarrass yourself in front of a customer, rather than dwell on your feelings try to say something funny, which may also help establish a rapport: *"Well, I wonder how many more things I can mess up today."* It's likely that the customer feels your embarrassment, so joking about it and then moving on will help you maintain your confidence. Another approach is to offer an explanation when appropriate: *"I apologize that I called you by the wrong name. When you came in, the sun blinded me and you looked like someone else."* And if you're the cause of the customer's embarrassment, always offer a phrase of regret followed by a phrase of empathy: *"I'm terribly sorry that I said that in front of other customers. I can imagine how that made you feel."*

Applying the Approach

When you or your customer is embarrassed, apply the following principles to your situations:

- If the customer did something, as in the example above, remind yourself that it wasn't done on purpose.
- Your goal is to quickly lessen the customer's feelings of embarrassment, so say something to show that you understand.

- Offer a phrase of empathy: *"I know how you feel."*

- Follow with a phrase of rapport: *"Yesterday I mistook one of my customers for another and launched into a conversation, only to realize my mistake when the customer stared blankly at me."*

- Use a humorous approach to help the customer get over the embarrassment: *"Imagine how I felt when I realized it was a different customer! The only thing I could do was to face it head on, so I said OOPS! You're not Bob. Thankfully, the customer had a sense of humor."*

- If you did something to embarrass your customer, offer a phrase of regret: *"I apologize that I did that to you."*

- Follow with a phrase of empathy: *"I'd understand if you're upset with me."*

- And if you did something to embarrass yourself, don't dwell on the situation, but rather say something to get the customer laughing: *"Geez, let me see if I can do this right. I've been doing things like this all day. I think I should go back home and start my day again!"*

What to Do When You're New and Not Yet Working Up to Speed

Everyone has been new on a job; therefore, everyone has been in your shoes and understands your feelings. You haven't yet developed confidence or found your comfort zone. You feel like a fish out of water. You're trying to handle your duties, get to know your coworkers and manager, and deal with customers all at the same time. Your coworkers and manager understand that you're new and should be helping you get up to speed. Your customers, on the other hand, don't have a clue that you're new. That is, until you begin helping them. You're working slowly. You're uncertain about how to handle their request. In addition, you're not fully familiar with the telephone, computer, or other equipment you're using to handle their request and, so, you just fumble along.

When you're new and not working up to speed, it may or may not be apparent to your customer. If you're handling the customer in person, he's likely to pick up on clues. Your facial expression and body language may signal that you're taking extra time because you're not sure what you're doing. If you're handling the customer by phone, she may wonder why it's taking you so long to handle the request. So talk about it. Don't be afraid to tell the customer why you're working slowly. Start by offering a phrase of regret: *"I apologize that it's taking me so long to handle this."* Follow with an explanation: *"I'm new and it takes me a little longer, but I want to make sure I do this correctly."* And because we've all been in your shoes, your explanation may also open the door to establishing a rapport. Your customer may respond: *"I can relate. It took me so long to learn my job,"* or *"No apology necessary. I've been there."*

Identifying the Customer's Response

When you're new, your customer may:

- Become frustrated by the amount of time you're taking.
- Wonder why it's taking so long.

- Not trust you to handle the request correctly.
- Want to involve a manager.
- Relate to your comments about being new.
- Understand and relax when he or she knows why you're not working faster.

Do This!

Erica is a new employee at a local bank. She recently completed teller training and, for the first week, her manager assigned another teller to shadow her. Today is her first day working on her own and she's extremely nervous. She feels as though she's forgotten everything she learned.

Employee: *"Good Morning. How may I help you?"* **(welcome)**

Customer: "I'd like to transfer funds from one account to another."

Employee: *"I'll be happy to help you with that. Have you completed the withdrawal and deposit forms?"* **(enthusiasm)**

Customer: "Geez, no, I haven't. Do you have blank forms?"

Employee: *"I sure do. Here you go."* **(enthusiasm)**

> (Erica handed the customer the forms and frantically tried to remember how to handle an account transfer. Her mind went blank. Then she took a deep breath, assured herself that she could do it, and thought about all the steps.)

Customer: "And here you go."

Employee: *"Thank you. I just got out of training last week. I'm sorry that it's taking me a little longer to handle this for you. I want to make sure I do all the steps correctly. This is the first transfer I've done so I'm going to review my notes as I go."* **(courtesy, rapport, regret, assurance)**

Customer: "Take all the time you need. I'm in no rush. I'm glad I can provide you with a training opportunity!"

Why This Works

When Erica's mind went blank, she calmed herself down and reminded herself that she could handle the customer's request. She offered a phrase of regret and explained why she was using her notes. Giving an explanation helped the customer to relate to what she was going through, the customer relaxed, and knowing the situation, told Erica to take her time, which also made Erica feel better.

Applying the Approach

When you're new and not working up to speed, apply the following principles to your situations:

- Don't be afraid to tell the customer why you're not working faster.
- Offer a phrase of regret, such as *"I apologize I'm not working faster."*
- Then explain your situation: *"This is my first day on the job."*
- Offering an explanation will often help you establish a rapport.
- Remind yourself that you can do this.
- Maintain a friendly (not worried) facial expression.
- Work as quickly as you're able and pay full attention to the task at hand.
- If you can't remember or figure out what to do, ask for help.
- Don't guess at an answer or try to figure out how to handle the request. If you don't know the answer or solution, ask a coworker.
- Remember that everyone has been in your shoes. Being new and not working up to speed is nothing to be ashamed of. It's more important to do the job correctly than to work quickly and come up with an incorrect resolution.

What to Do When You're Faced with an Ethical Dilemma

Throughout your career as a frontline employee, you're going to be confronted with choices. Many of those choices involve ethical decisions. It may be that your customer asks you to provide something special that you don't provide to all your customers, such as including an extra item at a reduced cost, expediting the delivery date, providing an item free of charge, or waiving a service fee. If you have a legitimate reason to bend the rules and provide these extras, such as satisfying a customer who was wronged by your company, then you have good reason to provide something special . . . after discussing the situation with your manager to ensure you have the authority to make that call.

But what happens when your customer tries to talk you into something that you feel will cross the ethical line? What happens if you comply and have that *what did I do* moment? If that happens, take responsibility and speak to your manager about it. Own up to the ethical dilemma you got yourself into. The safest bet, when it comes to ethical decisions, is to always speak to your manager first and let him or her make the call. When it comes to ethics, make sure you completely understand your company's position, as well as your authority limits. The best advice is to never make a decision that's ethically questionable to avoid an outcome that may not be positive for you.

Identifying the Customer's Response

When you're in an ethical dilemma, your customer may:

- Try to get you to comply with the request.
- Feel entitled to make other unethical demands in the future if you agree this time.

- Keep asking for more or continue to try to wear you down.
- Not be happy if he or she finds out that you gave special treatment to another customer.

Do This!

Lisa is a bartender in a trendy hotel restaurant. Her customers are often groups of convention attendees who are out to have a good time. While taking an order from a group of four men who were jovial and joking with her, one of the men took the joke too far and presented her with an ethical dilemma.

Customer: "Hey, if you forget to add this round of drinks to our tab, we'll more than make it up in your tip."

> (Lisa thought about the customer's request. Convention attendees were usually good tippers and, as a working mother, Lisa depended on her tips. The extra money would come in handy.)

Employee: *"Now that's a tempting offer, sir."* **(courtesy)**

Customer: "We'll definitely make it worth your while."

> (Lisa pondered it. After all, who would know? But then she thought about the consequences of complying with the request.)

Employee: *"Sir, as much as I'd like to, I'm sorry, but I'm not able to do that. As businessmen, you wouldn't want your employees doing something like that. I'm sure you understand why."* **(courtesy, regret, rapport, empathy)**

Customer: "No harm in asking, Miss. I appreciate your comment and yes, I understand completely."

Why This Works

It could have been an easy call for Lisa to agree with the customer and not charge for the round of drinks. No one would find out. But she knew that was the wrong decision and, even though the temptation was high, she made the right call. In speaking up, she used a phrase of empathy and the customer respected her for saying what she did. The bottom line is that whenever you're faced with an ethical dilemma, do the right thing. Had Lisa complied, and had her manager found out, she may have been fired. Even if her manager didn't find out, she would have known she crossed the line.

Applying the Approach

When you're faced with an ethical dilemma, apply the following principles to your situations:

- Always choose to do the right thing.
- If your customer tries talking you in to something unethical, offer a phrase of regret, such as *"I'm sorry. I'm not able to do that."*
- Follow with a phrase of empathy: *"I'm sure you understand why I can't do that."*
- Work on establishing a rapport: *"Some decisions are tough ones, but if you were in my situation you'd make the same call."*
- Maintain a positive attitude and a friendly demeanor.
- If you're unsure how to proceed, check with your manager.
- If you ever cross the ethical line, take responsibility and own up to your mistake with your boss.

What to Do When You Show That You're Having a Bad Day

You can be sailing along, everything's going smoothly, and you feel good about your life and your job. Then one day you're in a slump, angry about something, not feeling well, stressed out, or unable to put your finger on the reason why you're down. You just feel off your game; you're having a bad day. It happens to everyone. Even the most positive people don't feel positive every day. Sometimes they have to put forth extra effort to keep it together. The difference is that they're able put their feelings aside and act positive even when they're not feeling that way.

That's the best way to handle yourself when you're having a bad day, because your customers deserve to be treated well no matter how you're feeling. When you enter your workplace, leave your emotional baggage at the door. It may even be good to put aside what you're feeling inside for a while. Focus on your work and your customers. Remind yourself that everyone has a bad day now and then. It's how you handle those days that's important. Give yourself a pep talk.

It's not all right to show your customers through your actions or words that you're having a bad day, but you may do something that sends that message anyway. You may have a scowl on your face, your posture is slumped, or you don't make eye contact. Likewise, you may say something that conveys you're having a bad day. If this happens, offer a phrase of regret: *"Please forgive me. I'd like to start our conversation over."* It's not always necessary, but you may use this as an opportunity to establish a rapport: *"On the way to work a man cut me of. I had to slam on my brakes and almost hit his car. It really rattled me. I'm still trying to get that picture out of my mind but that was no reason to answer you as I did."* By offering a phrase of regret, you'll feel better. Now you can get yourself back on track and assist your customer.

Focus on your body language, on the words you choose, and pay complete attention to the customer.

Identifying the Customer's Response

When you show that you're having a bad day, your customer may:

- Hope that you handle the request correctly.
- Wonder if you're capable of handling the request.
- Want someone else to help.
- Wonder if you're like this every day.
- Feel sorry for you.

Do This!

Andrew works for a garden supply and landscape company. Normally his job is to be in the field, meeting with prospective clients to give estimates. Because another employee quit, he's been temporarily assigned to work in the store. He feels this is a setback, even though his boss explained that he needed Andrew to temporarily run the store until he hired someone new. Andrew dislikes being cooped inside, but he's handled his duties without complaining. Today, though, it came to a head. Early this morning a customer spoke in a condescending tone and made a negative comment about Andrew working in a garden center. The scene has been playing over and over in his mind and he's having a bad day. When another customer asked him a question, he didn't make eye contact, he was slumped over the counter, and he had scowl on his face.

Customer: "Excuse me, can you tell me where to find fertilizer for tomato plants?"
Employee: "Aisle 5."

(Andrew looked up after he spoke and noticed the customer looked at him oddly and then turned to walk away.)

Employee: *"I apologize for the way I said that. I'll be happy to show you where the fertilizer is and answer any questions you have."* **(regret, enthusiasm)**

Customer: "That'll be great, thanks."

Employee: *"When you asked me the question, I was still thinking about a negative comment a customer made to me earlier. I shouldn't have answered you as I did."* **(rapport)**

Customer: "The other day one of my customers got me so rattled it bothered me the rest of the day."

Why This Works

This approach worked because Andrew immediately recognized the inappropriate manner in which he spoke to this customer and he changed his attitude and demeanor. He apologized, offered a phrase of enthusiasm, and found a way to establish a rapport with the customer so that she knew why he had acted as he did. Because he was able to establish a rapport, he was able to put the previous situation out of his mind for the rest of the day.

Applying the Approach

When you show that you're having a bad day, apply the following principles to your situations:

- Remind yourself not to take your feelings out on your customers.
- Offer a phrase of regret when you've said or done something to show you're having a bad day, such as *"I feel so bad that I said that."*
- Offer a phrase of enthusiasm: *"I'll be happy to help you with that."*

- Work on establishing a rapport: *"My teenage son pushed my last button this morning and I'm trying to put that out of my mind."* Saying something like this in a joking manner will help you establish a rapport and you will most likely feel better too.

- Give yourself a pep talk.

- Try your best to put the situation out of your mind. If you start thinking about it, refocus your thoughts.

- Pay attention to your body language. Make sure you keep a friendly facial expression, maintain good posture, and an open demeanor.

- Make eye contact with your customers and pay full attention to them.

- Focus on maintaining a positive attitude for the rest of the day.

What to Do When You Feel You're Going to Lose It

A customer may push your buttons purposely to get a rise out of you, or may unwittingly say or do something that pushes your buttons. You're so upset you feel you're going to lose it. It could be a customer whose complaining is getting on your nerves, someone who won't stop nagging you, keeps making condescending comments, responds negatively to all your suggestions, is rude, argumentative, or just plain irritating. You feel your own irritation growing. You've had enough of this customer and wish he or she would just go away. You're ready to blow your cool and tell the customer off. Hopefully you won't do that.

When you feel your irritation growing and you feel you're going to lose it, stop, take a deep breath, and remind yourself it's your job to handle all types of customers, even those who push your buttons to the point you're ready to break. It's never okay to lash out or say something to show that you're about to lose your temper. Keep your cool and you keep the upper hand. Try to figure out why this customer is getting to you. If it's the customer's voice tone, this is probably part of this person's normal way of conversing and how he speaks to everyone. If you feel the customer is being sarcastic or nagging purposely, ask yourself: why is this customer doing this? Is she trying to wear you down or is she upset by something you said?

Try to view the situation from your customer's perspective. Often, a phrase of empathy can help: *"I get the impression that you're not happy with my answer. I understand it may not have been what you wanted to hear, but it's the best I can do."* Then you might try offering an explanation: *"The reason I'm not able to do that is. . . ."* By offering an explanation, you may redirect the conversation and help the customer view the situation from your perspective. Whether customers push your buttons on purpose or have no clue they're doing so, whenever you feel you're about to lose your patience, stay calm and in control, speak in a soft voice, and you'll be able to move through the interaction to a successful conclusion.

Identifying the Customer's Response

When you feel you're about to lose it, your customer may:

- Be trying to get an emotional reaction out of you.
- Be trying to upset you.
- Be trying to manipulate you.
- Be trying to get a rise out of you.
- Have no clue they're annoying you to the breaking point.

Do This!

Caroline works for a weight loss center. One of her job duties is to lead weekly meetings at which clients share their success stories and can ask for help with problems they're having. Last week one of the clients, Diana, arrived early while Caroline was setting up the room. She chattered on and on to the point that Caroline got sidetracked and couldn't think straight. She counted on this time to review her agenda and plan how she was going to lead the meetings. To make matters worse, during the meeting Diana dominated the conversation, and Caroline felt she didn't do a good job leading because no one else had a chance to speak. Caroline was annoyed and tonight as she was starting to set up the room, Diana again strolled in and began talking. Caroline is about ready to lose it. She wants to tell Diana to just shut up already.

Client: "I'm so proud of myself. I lost three pounds this week. I've been really good about making better choices. I've also been exercising every day too. . . ."

(As soon as Caroline felt her annoyance boiling over, she stopped, took a deep breath, and looked at the situation from Diana's perspective.)

Employee: *"Diana, I can tell how proud you feel. I'm excited for you that you're doing so well."* **(courtesy, empathy, enthusiasm)**

Client: "Oh, thanks. I'm doing really well. Monday I walked two miles, Tuesday I rode my bike, Wednesday I tried a new exercise class. . . ."

> (Caroline felt the hair rising on the nape of her neck, knowing that Diana wasn't about to stop talking. Besides, she knew she was going to hear it all again during the meeting. Again, she took a deep breath and calmed herself down.)

Employee: *"I really appreciate your sharing this with me, and I can tell you're very excited. Right now, though, I'm trying to gather my thoughts about what I'm going to say during the meeting. Do you mind waiting until that time, please? I'm going to give everyone a chance to share their success stories and when I call on you I'll be thrilled to hear your good news."* **(appreciation, courtesy, assurance)**

Client: "I'm so sorry. I didn't mean to interrupt you."

Employee: *"Diana, no apology is necessary. It's just that if I don't review my agenda, I'm afraid I won't be an effective leader. Thanks for being so understanding."* **(courtesy)**

Why This Works

Even though Caroline was irritated by Diana's droning, she held it together and was able to calm herself down. She reminded herself that Diana wasn't purposely trying to annoy her. Caroline was able to view the situation from Diana's perspective and understood why she was so excited. She offered a phrase of empathy and one of enthusiasm. When Diana continued to drone on, Caroline politely asked if she'd mind holding her thoughts until the meeting and explained why she was asking that. By staying calm and in control, she was able to change the direction of the conversation and the outcome was positive. She felt proud of herself for handling the situation calmly.

Quick Tip for a Sticky Situation

When your customer chatters on and the noise is keeping you from doing your job, as in Caroline's case, if you feel you're about to lose control of your emotions, offering a phrase of empathy and then politely explaining why you need the quiet time is the best way to handle the situation: *"I can see how you feel and I'd like to hear more about it. Will you mind holding your thoughts for just a moment while I enter the information on my computer?"* Adding a bit of humor can also help: *"I hate to admit it, but I haven't yet learned how to do two things at once."*

Applying the Approach

When you feel you're ready to lose it, apply the following principles to your situations:

- Number 1 rule: stay calm and in control of your emotions.
- Try to figure out the reason the customer is pushing your buttons. Is he doing it on purpose? Is the annoying trait part of her personality?
- Take a deep breath.
- Maintain your positive attitude.
- Keep a friendly facial expression.
- Speak with a helpful tone of voice.
- Offer a phrase of empathy if you feel it'll help the customer change the dialogue, such as *"I understand how you feel and I wish I could do more."*
- Work through the steps of your interaction, trying your best to ignore what the customer is saying or doing.
- End the interaction with a phrase of appreciation: *"I'm glad I was able to help you today."*
- Give yourself a pat on the back that you didn't let the customer know your buttons were pushed.

What to Do When You're Having a Personal Problem That Affects Your Work

You may be going through an extremely tough time in your life. It's a huge problem that's affecting your work. It's almost too much to handle, yet you try. You come to work every day, hoping to put it out of your mind. You can't. As hard as you try to maintain a positive demeanor, you're afraid it shows. If you're in this situation and afraid it shows, it most likely does.

So how do you work when you're going through an extremely tough time? Talk to your manager about the situation. Explain that something is going on and it's affecting your work: "I'm having a personal problem that's beginning to affect my work. Today I almost snapped at a rude customer. I was able to hold it together but after I finished my call, I had to take a short break. I don't want it to affect my job, and I felt it was important to talk to you about it. I'm trying really hard to rein in my emotions but I'm afraid I'm going to lose it." Although it's important to discuss the situation with your manager, you don't have to provide all the details unless you feel comfortable. Perhaps your manager can temporarily assign you to other job duties or offer some advice that can be helpful. The most important thing to remember is that trying to keep a personal problem bottled up inside is bound to end up with the problem spilling over and affecting your work. And if you work with customers, you never want to take that chance.

Identifying the Customer's Response

When you feel you're having a personal problem that's affecting your work, your customer may:

- Become upset if you don't handle the request effectively or efficiently.

- Ask for someone else to handle the request.
- Ask to speak to a supervisor.
- Pick up on your emotional state and ask what's wrong.

Do This!

Alex works in a sporting goods store as a sales associate. He's been trained to work in every department and is the go-to person when his coworkers and customers need help. He's proud of his accomplishments and is on a fast-track to be promoted to manager. But his personal life is a mess. He's been married for three years, has a two-year-old child, and his wife announced last week that she wants a divorce. Alex was blindsided by the news, and although his wife agreed to try counseling, his emotions have been all over the place. He's trying to hold it together but this morning he and his wife got into a huge fight and he doesn't know how he's going to make it through the day. As soon as he got to work, he knew it would be best if he talked to his manager.

Employee: "I'm having a personal problem at home and although I don't yet feel comfortable talking about it, I wanted to let you know about it. Since last week I've been having a tough time holding it together. This morning something happened and I'm not sure how I'm going to make it through the day."

Manager: "Gee, I'm sorry to hear that, Alex. You've done a good job keeping it inside. I had no clue anything was wrong. I understand you don't want to discuss the details but anytime you need to talk to someone, I'm here for you. If you feel you need the day off, that's fine."

Employee: "No, actually I feel better being here. But is there another job I can do today where I won't have to deal with customers?"

Manager: "Absolutely. I've got a job in the stockroom I can have you do."

Employee: "Thanks so much. I don't want to cause a problem and if I feel I can handle customers later today I'll let you know."

Manager: "No problem. I'll help you in whatever way I can."

Why This Works

This scenario worked on two counts. Number one, Alex was up front, dealt with his situation head-on, and spoke to his manager. Number two, he worked for a manager who cared about the welfare of his employees and was willing to work with Alex. Whether or not your manager is as caring as Alex's, it's important to share what's going on whenever you have a personal problem that may impede your ability to handle your customers well. Had Alex not said anything, he may have made a mistake or spoken inappropriately to a customer.

Applying the Approach

When you're having a personal problem that affects your work, apply the following principles to your situations:

- Sometimes you'll be able to put aside your personal problems; working can be the best medicine as takes your mind off your situation for a while.

- Whether or not you feel that you'll be able to handle your job duties to the best of your ability, it's your responsibility to let your manager know.

- Find a private space and discuss your situation with your manager.

- You don't have to provide all the details, only enough information so that your manager can make sense of your situation, as Alex did.

- Depending on your relationship with your manager, he or she may be understanding or quite the opposite. No matter your relationship, you owe it to your company and to your customers to speak up when you know your ability to work well is in jeopardy.

- If you must continue to interact with customers, do your best to focus on them, try to pay complete attention, and handle your interactions to the best of your ability.

- After each interaction, check your work to make sure you handled everything correctly.

6

Powerful Phrases for Social Media Interactions

hen Shakespeare wrote "All the World's a Stage," he had no idea that one day his words would take on a literal meaning. That one day is today. That stage is called social media. Everyone now has a global stage, and the business community is looking for ways to jump on board, to keep pace with the impact that social media is having on customer interactions, particularly in the area of customer service. Consumers, eager to voice their opinions, are holding companies accountable through social media. They use these sites to post random comments and pay compliments, but most often, to voice their complaints. When they voice complaints, their voice often grows exponentially stronger when others join in. That strong voice holds corporations accountable for their actions, and some companies have even succumbed to public pressure and changed their policies. Power to the People!

As a consumer, you may have used social media sites to post a comment, pay a compliment, or perhaps to voice a complaint. You're in the customer service business, so you're keenly aware of how it feels to be on the receiving end of service, both good and bad. You may have posted a compliment about an employee. You may have been upset about service you received and felt compelled to log on to a social media site and say what you wanted to say. After voicing your complaint, you probably felt empowered that you were able to voice your thoughts on a very public medium. Power to you!

As a consumer, you understand why people like to voice their thoughts on social media sites. As a customer service provider, however, you're also on the other side of the coin. You're responsible for ensuring that each of your customers is satisfied with the service they received. You know that if a customer is dissatisfied, he or she can access a social networking site and carp about the experience, even naming you as the culprit if space allows! So it's even more crucial that you pay attention to the powerful phrases you learned and incorporate phrases of welcome, courtesy, rapport, enthusiasm, assurance, empathy, regret, and appreciation into every interaction.

Wouldn't you rather read a post: spoke to (you). Awesome rep. Resolved my billing problem. Thanks! than read: spoke to (you). Awful rep. Bad attitude. No help resolving bill problem. Didn't even listen. Either way, everyone at your company, not to mention the global community, knows how this customer feels about the service you provided. Of course, the post may or may not be accurate, and you or the employee assigned to handle social media contacts will have the opportunity to respond. But now that you're incorporating powerful phrases into your conversations, you increase the odds that customers will only post positive comments about you.

The intent of this chapter isn't to teach you how to establish a social media presence or to monitor and manage social media. We'll assume that someone in your customer service department is in charge of monitoring social media. Rather, this chapter is designed to help you handle customers through social media interactions.

The good news is that everything you've learned in this book can be translated into written form. If you're responsible for handling social media customer service and receive a comment or compliment, you'll correspond with the customer via the social media site. But when it comes to handling complaints, social media will never replace old fashioned customer service, and that's done through traditional voice interaction. If you receive a complaint, you'll want to immediately offer a phrase of regret in writing, but then handle the customer by phone or in person to resolve the issue.

This chapter focuses on three scenarios: customer comments, complaints, and compliments. You'll learn how to initially respond via the social medium outlet and how to handle the balance of the interaction when additional follow up is required. Each behavior and the appropriate approach is identified with examples, along with a *Do This!* scenario containing pertinent written dialogue. You'll learn which powerful phrases to use so that you will be able to apply the approach to your particular work environment and your customer interactions. The powerful phrases are denoted in *italics* with the type powerful phrase noted in (**bold**).

What to Do When a Customer Makes a Comment

Some people use social media sites to vent complaints when service is particularly awful or to pay compliments when service is surprisingly better than expected. Then there are people who use social media as a communication tool to comment on their daily goings on, even if the goings on are run of the mill or mundane. Customers may make a random comment about a product your company offers, or the layout of your store, or compare you to your competition, just to name a few examples. Some people just like to "talk."

When that "talk" is about your company on a social media site and it's your job to respond, do you have to respond to every comment? That's your company's call, but from a customer service perspective, why not? Engaging your social media customers will keep them interested in your company and makes the business relationship more personal. Besides, it won't take long to formulate your response, and responding to every comment lets your customers know that you're paying attention. Just make sure that you check your response before sending and edit if appropriate. Remember that "All the World's a Stage"; therefore, whatever you send out may be seen around the globe. When a customer makes a comment about your company on a social media site, offer phrases of enthusiasm and appreciation: *Glad you found what you were looking for at our store. We appreciate your business.* Even when customers make random comments, showing your appreciation that they bought from you shows that you're listening and that you care about them.

Identifying the Customer's Response

A customer may make a comment about:

- A specific product.
- The variety of products.
- The layout of your business.
- The location of your business.
- A comparison between you and your competition.

Do This!

Hank works as a customer service specialist in the corporate office of a home improvement chain. Although a specialized team is responsible for monitoring and managing social media content, he's been assigned to respond to the comments and interact with the customers. His manager just handed him the following customer comment:

Customer: Just bought a power drill at Handyman's Station. so many choices. chose the Mac200. hope I like it.

(After reading the comment, Hank formulates the following response.)

Employee: *The Mac200 is our most popular drill & we hear good things about it.* **(enthusiasm)**

(He's ready to send the message but after rereading it, he decides to add more.)

Employee: *The Mac200 is our most popular drill & we hear good things about it. Thanks for buying it at Handyman's Station!* **(enthusiasm, appreciation)**

(Hank's happy with the complete response. He sends the message.)

Why This Works

The team responsible for monitoring social media may have read this random comment about the power drill and decided not to respond. But the person who made the decision that the company should respond to all social media comments made a wise decision. It didn't take Hank long to formulate his response and taking this quick action showed that this company appreciated each of its customers.

Applying the Approach

When responding to a social media comment, apply the following principles to your situations:

- Respond quickly.
- Offer a phrase of enthusiasm, such as, *Glad you like the layout of our store.*
- Follow with a phrase of appreciation: *Thanks for your business. We appreciate you!*
- Read your response before sending out, and edit if necessary.
- Remember that anything you post is out there for everyone to see.
- Never post anything personal about yourself.
- If you're responsible for creating miscellaneous outgoing posts, think of unique ways to keep your customers interested and engaged. Try a contest, post a trivia question or a thought for the day (relating to your company), offer a coupon to your followers, or ask customers their thoughts on a specific product, service, or how you can improve.

What to Do When a Customer Complains

Consumers are holding companies accountable for service. When they're not happy, voicing a complaint on a social networking site gives them a sense of control, even a sense of power over the company. When a customer uses social media to voice a complaint, the whole world may see it. Complaining via a social networking site may well be your company's worst case scenario: that is, unless you respond quickly and respond thoughtfully. Customers who complain through these media do so to see if and how you're going to respond. And they want you to respond. They want action. They want their complaints dealt with. Look at these complaints as a gift: customers are giving you the opportunity to make things right, and the added benefit is that you have an opportunity to show the whole world that you care about resolving complaints quickly and correctly.

The downside of complaining via social media is that the customer may not give an accurate version of what happened. Anyone can say anything, and it's your job to get to the bottom of the complaint and deal with the customer whether or not the complaint is legitimate. Whenever a customer complains, handle the complaint as though you were handling the customer in person or by phone. Immediately offer a phrase of regret: *I'm sorry we didn't meet your expectations.* Follow up with a phrase of assurance: *I'm going to look into this immediately.* If it's a simple fix that can be answered in a reply post, respond: *we're aware of the phone problem. Should be resolved any minute now.* But if you need more information, say so: *I need to get the details to resolve this.* In this scenario, you'll want to handle the complaint by speaking with the customer rather than continuing the online banter: *My name is Natalie. Please call me at 800-500-0000, ext 100.* If space allows, offer a phrase of appreciation: *We appreciate the opportunity to make this right.* Now your customer (and anyone reading the post) will know that you care about resolving the problem. That's really all your customers want. When something goes wrong, they want it righted.

Identifying the Customer's Response

A customer may complain about:

- Trouble accessing your website.
- Trouble using a product.
- An unresolved problem.
- Frustration in dealing with your company or an employee.
- Frustration in trying to reach an employee by telephone.
- Frustration in using your website.
- Anything they'd complain about in person or on the phone.
- Anything to get their voice heard.

Do This!

Because Hank works in the corporate office, he primarily handles customers who are extremely dissatisfied with the company. And, because he's responsible for handling customer contacts on social networking sites, those contacts are most often complaints. His job is to get to the root of the problem and then work with the store or department to resolve the issue, while maintaining contact with the customer, and following up until the problem is resolved. Hank's manager handed him the following complaint:

Customer: Waiting for a backorder item for 3 mo. No one can tell me anything. Sick of dealing with them. No one cares.

(Hank read the customer's complaint. He needed a lot more information. Which store was involved? What was the backordered item? Was the customer's complaint even legitimate?)

Employee: *So sorry this happened. My name is Hank & I'm going to look into this. Call me at 888-300-3000 ext 300. Need details.* **(regret, assurance)**

Customer: Thanks Hank. At least someone cares!

(Hank then handled the balance of the contact over the phone. He identified the customer's behavior as agitated and handled the contact appropriately. He spoke to the store manager and then contacted the vendor. He called the customer back with the date the item would be available and said that he'd follow up with a phone call on that date just to be sure the item was in stock. Because of the customer's frustration and the store employees' lack of proper handling, he also sent the customer a twenty dollar gift card for his inconvenience. Then Hank responded through the social network channel.)

Employee: *So glad I was able to resolve your problem. We value your business and I hope I restored your faith in Handyman's Station.* **(enthusiasm, appreciation)**

Customer: Thanks Hank! You did! Great job!

Why This Works

Even though Hank knew none of the details, including whether or not the complaint was valid, he immediately responded via the social network site and offered a phrase of regret, followed by a phrase of assurance that he was going to handle the problem. But he also needed more information, so he asked the customer to call him directly. He was then able to handle the situation over the phone and resolve the problem to the customer's satisfaction. Because of the customer's agitation in dealing with the local store, Hank went a step further and sent a gift card for a future purchase, which also helped restore the customer's faith in Handyman's Station. Hank finalized the contact by responding through the social media site so that anyone reading the customer's post would know the problem had been resolved. And because Hank felt the store did not handle the customer well, he referred the situation to his manager, who would speak to the local store manager to determine what additional steps should be taken to avoid a repetition of this type of complaint.

Applying the Approach

When responding to a social media complaint, apply the following principles to your situations:

- Immediately respond with a phrase of regret, such as, *We're so sorry.*

- If you're aware of the problem and can address it in your response, add a phrase of appreciation: *We value your business and are working to fix the problem with our website. Will be fixed within an hour.*

- If you need more time to investigate, include a phrase of assurance: *I'm going to check on this right now.*

- If you need additional information, ask the customer to call or state that you'll call the customer: *Need more info. Please call me at. . . .*

- Try to figure out the type of challenging behavior: is the customer angry, confused, combative? Once you determine the type of behavior, you'll be able to handle the interaction well when you speak to the customer.

- If the customer has no basis for the complaint, remember that what you write can be seen by anyone so choose your words carefully. Don't write something such as, You don't know what you're talking about. We don't even carry that product. Instead, write, *I'm sorry for your frustration in trying to order that, but we don't carry that product. Wish I could help.* Same message, different manner of speaking. You got your point across but said it in a respectful way.

- Never say anything negative. Period.

- If the customer refuses your offer to resolve the complaint and won't provide specific details, be sure to address this in your response, including phrases of appreciation and assurance: *We value your business, but the only way I can fix this is by speaking to you to get the details. I wish you'd call me.*

What to Do When a Customer Compliments

You know that customers are much more likely to complain than to compliment; however, social media has made it easier for people to shout out a rave about a company, product, or employee since they can do it in a few characters and from the convenience of their homes. Customers may be so delighted with the great service they received that they'll post an online compliment about the employee who went above and beyond. Some people may post a positive review about a product, while others post generic compliments with the hopes of receiving a perk from the business. If you're the employee assigned to respond to social media, responding to a compliment will be your easiest task.

Usually, follow up won't be necessary. All you'll need to do is respond with a phrase of appreciation: *Thank you for your comments about Shannon. We appreciate hearing from you.* If you plan to do internal follow through, you'll want to let the customer know: *We think she's great too and will pass your post to her manager.* It's that simple. If someone posts a compliment about a product or service: *Absolutely love my pitching wedge. Totally improved my golf game. Awesome!* Respond with phrases of enthusiasm and appreciation: *Terrific! Thanks for letting us know.* You may also use compliments to engage other customers by asking their opinions that pertain to the initial compliment. Or you may want to see if you can turn a customer's compliment into additional sales. You decide to offer a coupon and change your response to: *Terrific! Thanks for letting us know-we're sending you a $10 coupon. Everyone ordering the pitching wedge today gets the coupon with their order.* Leveraging a customer's compliment into a marketing opportunity can be very good for your business. If you're the person assigned to responding to social media and your company isn't identifying marketing opportunities, suggest it to your boss or the social media management team.

Identifying the Customer's Response

A customer may post a compliment about:

- Quick turnaround.
- Unexpected service.
- A specific employee.
- A specific product.
- The variety of products you offer.
- Appreciation for your company in general.

Do This!

Hank is given the following compliment to handle:

Customer: Love your stores. So many products, I can always find what I want at Handyman's Station.

Employee: *Thanks for letting us know! We pride ourselves in offering a wide variety of products at the lowest possible cost.* **(appreciation)**

> (Hank used the compliment to take advantage of sending a positive message about his company. But then he thought of a way to turn the post into a market research opportunity. After speaking to his manager, he changed his response.)

Employee: *Thanks! We're entering you into a drawing. . . . Who loves us? Everyone, tell us why and you'll be entered into a drawing for a $25 gc.* **(appreciation)**

Why This Works

Hank found a way to turn the compliment into a marketing opportunity. Not only did he show appreciation to the customer for posting the compliment, he took advantage of that and created a special drawing that will provide useful consumer information for his company and also make the winner of the drawing very happy.

Applying the Approach

When responding to a social media compliment, apply the following principles to your situations:

- Offer a phrase of appreciation, such as, *Thanks so much for letting us know!*

- Look for opportunities to post a positive comment about your company: *We value each of our customers by offering a wide range of services. Thanks!*

- Engaging other customers to post their thoughts is a way of learning more about who your customers are and why they choose your business, which will provide valuable market research information.

- If the compliment specifies an employee, pass the information to the employee's manager.

- Look for ways to leverage a compliment into a marketing opportunity by offering a special discount, a coupon, or a drawing.

- When engaging customers, ask your question in a way to encourage other positive posts: *Tell us why you like this product & we'll enter your name into a drawing for a gift card.*